A first course in the essentials of
Grammar

BOOKS BY HAROLD LEVINE

English Alive
English: A Comprehensive Course
Comprehensive English Review Text
Vocabulary for the College-Bound Student
Vocabulary for the High School Student
Vocabulary Through Pleasurable Reading, Books I and II
Vocabulary and Composition Through Pleasurable Reading,
    Books III, IV, V, and VI

When ordering this book, please specify
either **R 239 W** *or*
ENGLISH ALIVE WORKBOOK (GRAMMAR)

Dedicated to serving

AMSCO

our nation's youth

ENGLISH ALIVE

Harold Levine

AMSCO SCHOOL PUBLICATIONS, INC.

315 Hudson Street / New York, N.Y. 10013

ISBN 0-87720-426-8

Printed in the United States of America

A Conversation Between Student and Author

STUDENT: Why do I need this book?

AUTHOR: It will give you a solid foundation in a subject that you, a user of English, will need for the rest of your life—grammar.

STUDENT: I haven't understood grammar too well in the past. What makes you think this book is going to help me?

AUTHOR: The main concern of this book is you, the learner. Every sentence in it, every word, has been examined and reexamined with these thoughts in mind:
> Will it be clear to *you?*
> Will *you* understand it?
> Is it going to help *you?*

No language likely to confuse you or discourage you from learning has been permitted between the covers of this book.

The book consists of short lessons. A typical lesson begins by getting you interested and showing you the value of learning what the lesson has to teach.

When a lesson uses a term for the first time—for example, *singular, plural, vowel, consonant,* etc.—it explains as clearly as possible what the term means. Nothing is taken for granted.

When a lesson introduces a topic, it raises questions that are likely to be in your mind, and it answers these questions.

When a lesson asks you to do an exercise, it helps by answering some of the first questions for you as samples, so that you will know exactly what to do.

As you work on the short, yet challenging, lessons in this book, either by yourself or in class with your teacher, you will probably be surprised at your progress in a subject that may have turned you off in the past.

STUDENT: Am I required to have studied any other book before using this book?

AUTHOR: No.

STUDENT: Is there anything else in the book besides grammar?

AUTHOR: Yes. There are composition hints that teach you how to express yourself in fewer words, without repetition, and with greater effectiveness. There are lessons that help you improve your spelling, punctuation, and other important English skills.

STUDENT: This book is probably too hard for me.

AUTHOR: That is not so. Just turn to the beginning of the book and try the first lesson or two. In this way you can discover for yourself how easy and pleasurable it can be to learn from *English Alive*.

A Word to the Teacher

I have organized this first course in the essentials of grammar into lessons. Each lesson consists of instruction that average students should be able to deal with successfully in a single classroom period. Brighter students, of course, may be able to do a lesson in less than a period, and some of the slower ones may need two periods.

In each lesson I have tried to provide motivation, clear examples, practical applications, and abundant, varied exercises. I hope you and your students enjoy using the book.

Harold Levine

Acknowledgments

The author wishes to thank Norman Levine (City College of the City University of New York) and Robert T. Levine (North Carolina A & T State University) for their valuable assistance as consultants and critics, and the editorial staff of Amsco School Publications for their editing and encouragement.

CONTENTS

lesson 1 Complete and Incomplete Sentences

A *complete sentence* is a group of words that expresses a complete thought.

Let us consider whether the following are complete or incomplete sentences:

1. At six in the morning.

> (What happens, or will happen, or has happened *at six in the morning?* We are not told. The thought is not complete.)　　(INCOMPLETE SENTENCE)

2. At six in the morning, the newspapers are delivered.

> (This is much better. We are told what happens *at six in the morning.* The thought is complete.)　　(COMPLETE SENTENCE)

3. I am leaving at six in the morning.

> (This is fine, too. We are told what is going to happen *at six in the morning.* The thought is complete.)　　(COMPLETE SENTENCE)

Question:　Is it ever correct to use an incomplete sentence?

Answer:　Yes, especially in conversation.

For example, suppose you are planning to leave on a trip at six in the morning, and a friend asks, "When are you leaving?" What would your answer be?

You surely would not say, "I am leaving at six in the morning." The words *I am leaving* are understood. They do not have to be said.

The only natural answer in these circumstances would be the incomplete sentence, "At six in the morning."

Caution:　You may use incomplete sentences in ordinary everyday conversation, but not in formal writing. By *formal writing*, we mean reports, letters of application, answers to essay questions on examinations, etc.

In formal writing, use complete sentences.

What is wrong with the following?

1. **Because it was a holiday.**

    (So what happened? We are not told.) (INCOMPLETE SENTENCE)

    I slept late because it was a holiday. (COMPLETE SENTENCE)

2. **Expecting a phone call.**

    (We are not told who was expecting a phone call.) (INCOMPLETE SENTENCE)

    Cindy was expecting a phone call. (COMPLETE SENTENCE)

3. **If he is not invited.**

    (We are not told what he will do if he is not invited.) (INCOMPLETE SENTENCE)

    He will not come if he is not invited. (COMPLETE SENTENCE)

4. **Before the half was over.**

    (What happened before the half was over? This information is not given.) (INCOMPLETE SENTENCE)

    We tied the score before the half was over. (COMPLETE SENTENCE)

EXERCISE 1. If the group of words is a complete sentence, write **C.S.** in the space at the left. If it is an incomplete sentence, write **I.S.**

_____ 1. Fell off a skateboard.

_____ 2. For lunch we had spaghetti and cheese.

_____ 3. The parking field in back of the supermarket.

_____ 4. Erica coughed.

_____ 5. When Carlos got on base.

_____ 6. Before my visit to the dentist.

_____ 7. Before dinner I watched TV.

_____ 8. Her name is Helen.

_____ 9. With cole slaw and potato salad.

_____ 10. When the bus stopped, we got off.

_____ 11. The second Saturday in June.

_____ 12. The bakery on the corner is open.

_____ 13. Skiing is exciting.

_____ 14. For Herman's birthday.

_____ 15. Though I was very tired.

_____ 16. When Susan ran for office, I voted for her.

_____ 17. The sneakers had torn laces.

_____18. Stopped at a gas station to ask for directions.

_____19. Sheldon called.

_____20. Waiting for a chance to play.

EXERCISE 2. Which way of finishing the sentence will result in a complete sentence? Write your answer in the space provided.

Samples:

The girl ___*bought a bag of popcorn*_____.

sitting next to your sister   bought a bag of popcorn
we met on the bus   who sang the anthem

___*We live*_____ around the corner.

The shop   In a lot
We live   An accident

1. The shirt _____.

in the top drawer   that he wore yesterday
has no pockets   bought at Macy's

2. _____ about four in the afternoon.

They came   No later than
A loud noise   Arriving

3. As I looked out the window _____.

to see what was going on   and the sun was shining
of the living room   , a patrol car drove up

4. _____ watching the game.

Many people were   While you were
After several minutes of   On TV

5. Outside the house _____.

that was just sold   where Alan lives
playing ball   painters were at work

6. _____ when you get to the end of the bridge.

If you turn right   Because there is construction
You must pay a toll   In heavy traffic

7. The door _____.

to the garage   at the rear of the building
that was forced open   is always locked

8. _____ tickets.

    Because they had no   Vera bought two
    If we show our   Stood on line to buy

9. Without _____.

    going into a long story   waiting for the light to change
    food we cannot live   enough money to buy the watch

10. Swimming _____.

    like a fish   is good exercise
    the length of the pool   at the seashore

lesson 2 Declarative and Interrogative Sentences

Question: What do we use a sentence for?

Answer: We use a sentence to

> *make a statement,* or
> *ask a question,* or
> *express a command or request,* or
> *express strong feeling.*

In this lesson we will deal with sentences that make statements and sentences that ask questions.

I. DECLARATIVE SENTENCES

A sentence that makes a statement is called a *declarative sentence*.

Plants need sunlight.	(DECLARATIVE SENTENCE)
Mona lost an earring.	(DECLARATIVE SENTENCE)
All the tickets were sold.	(DECLARATIVE SENTENCE)

Most sentences are declarative sentences.

Punctuation: A declarative sentence ends with a period [.].

EXERCISE 1. Write declarative sentences beginning with the words below.

Samples:

The dog's name ___*is Flash.*_____

I ___*came early.*_____

Andy ___*knows the answer.*_____

1. My friend's name _____

2. We _____

3. A cat _____

4. The door _____

5. George Washington _____

6. The windows _____

7. Our team _____

8. She _____

9. The room _____

10. You _____

Reminder: **Did you end each sentence with a period?**

II. INTERROGATIVE SENTENCES

A sentence that asks a question is called an *interrogative sentence*.

Do plants need sunlight?   (INTERROGATIVE SENTENCE)
Did Mona lose an earring?   (INTERROGATIVE SENTENCE)
Were all the tickets sold?   (INTERROGATIVE SENTENCE)

Punctuation: An interrogative sentence ends with a question mark [?].

EXERCISE 2. Write interrogative sentences beginning with the words below.

Samples:

Did you ___*find your keys?*___

Is the book ___*interesting?*___

Are your friends ___*coming to the game?*___

1. Did your brother _____

2. Is the soup _____

3. Are they _____

4. Was the trip _____

5. Do we _____

6. Were the neighbors _____

7. Does the story _____

8. Should I _____

9. Has the rain _____

10. Will the driver _____

Reminder: **Did you end each sentence with a question mark?**

EXERCISE 3. Change the following declarative sentences to interrogative sentences.

Samples:

The price is high.

Is the price high?

Refreshments will be served.

Will refreshments be served?

We won the game.

Did we win the game?

1. The butter is fresh.

2. Checks will be accepted.

3. She finished on time.

4. The gates are open.

5. Our expenses have increased.

6. Your turn will come soon.

7. The light was green.

8. Fred has returned.

9. They would like some more cake.

10. Julia plays tennis.

Reminder: **Did you end each sentence with a question mark?**

lesson 3 Imperative and Exclamatory Sentences

I. IMPERATIVE SENTENCES

A sentence that expresses a command or makes a request is called an *imperative sentence*.

Answer the phone.	(IMPERATIVE SENTENCE—COMMAND)
Pass the butter, please.	(IMPERATIVE SENTENCE—REQUEST)
Get out of here this minute!	(IMPERATIVE SENTENCE—COMMAND)

Punctuation: An imperative sentence ends with a period [.], but when it expresses strong feeling, it ends with an exclamation point [!].

You is understood in an imperative sentence. When we say *Answer the phone*, we mean *You answer the phone*. When we say *Pass the butter, please*, we mean *You pass the butter, please*.

EXERCISE 1. Change the following imperative sentences to interrogative sentences.

Samples:

Open the door.	*Will you open the door?*
Please pay the cashier.	*Will you please pay the cashier?*

1. Have some more pie. _____
2. Please wait. _____
3. Sit down. _____
4. Continue. _____
5. Look out! _____
6. Kindly step this way. _____
7. Hold my books, please. _____
8. Pardon my interruption. _____

Reminder: Did you end each of the above sentences with a question mark?

EXERCISE 2.   Change the following interrogative sentences to imperative sentences.

Samples:

Will you watch your step, please?   _*Watch your step, please.*_____

Can you be on time?   _*Be on time.*_____

1. Will you close the window, please?   _____
2. Will you be careful?   _____
3. Could you come back later?   _____
4. Will you stop?   _____
5. Can you say something?   _____

> *Reminder:*   **Imperative sentences end with a period or an exclamation point. Check your punctuation of the above sentences.**

II.   EXCLAMATORY SENTENCES

A sentence that expresses strong feeling is called an *exclamatory sentence*.

What a mistake I made!   (EXCLAMATORY SENTENCE)
How lucky she was!   (EXCLAMATORY SENTENCE)
You were amazing!   (EXCLAMATORY SENTENCE)

Exclamatory sentences often begin with *What* or *How*.

Punctuation: An exclamatory sentence ends with an exclamation point [!].

EXERCISE 3.   What exclamatory sentence would you use in the following situations?

Samples:

To tell someone what a wonderful time you had at the beach:

   *What a wonderful time I had at the beach!*_____

To tell a friend how lovely she looks in her new outfit:

   *How lovely you look in your new outfit!*_____

1. To express disgust at what a fool you were yesterday:

   _____

2. To tell your family how good it is to be home:

   _____

3. To tell a teammate what a fine catch he or she made:

_____

4. To tell a friend what a horrible movie you saw yesterday:

_____

5. To tell people indoors how cold it is outside:

_____

Reminder: **Did you end each of the above sentences with an exclamation point?**

EXERCISE 4. (*Review*) Punctuate the following sentences by adding a period, question mark, or exclamation point at the end of each sentence. Also indicate whether the sentence is *declarative, interrogative, imperative,* or *exclamatory.*

Sample:

Are you ready__?__   _interrogative_____

1. How clever you were____   _____
2. How old is Joe's brother____   _____
3. Cats are intelligent____   _____
4. Have some more soda____   _____
5. Was Christopher Columbus Italian____ _____
6. What a wonderful time we had____ _____
7. What is your address____   _____
8. I can't stop the car____   _____
9. Marie Curie was born in Poland____ _____
10. Please help me carry these books____ _____

EXERCISE 5. (*Review*) Write sentences of your own, as directed below. Remember, of course, to begin each sentence with a *capital* (large) letter.

Sample:

Sentence that makes a statement:

   The shortest month of the year is February.

1. Sentence that makes a request:

_____

2. Sentence that expresses a command:

_____

3. Sentence that asks a question:

_____

4. Sentence that expresses strong feeling:

_____

5. Sentence that makes a statement:

_____

    Reminder: (1) **Did you begin each sentence with a capital letter?**

                 (2) **Did you end each sentence with the proper punctuation?**

lesson 4 The Subject

A sentence has two parts: (1) a *subject* and (2) a *predicate*. This lesson will deal with the subject.

The *subject* is the part of the sentence about which something is told or asked.

The seats on the bus are very comfortable.

> QUESTION: About what is the sentence telling something?
>
> ANSWER: *The seats on the bus.*
>
> SUBJECT: *The seats on the bus.*

Amelia Earhart disappeared over the Pacific.

> QUESTION: About whom is the sentence telling something?
>
> ANSWER: *Amelia Earhart.*
>
> SUBJECT: *Amelia Earhart.*

Has your brother Tom found a job?

> QUESTION: About whom is the sentence asking something?
>
> ANSWER: *your brother Tom.*
>
> SUBJECT: *your brother Tom.*

Position of the Subject

The subject is usually found at the beginning of the sentence, but it can also appear in other positions.

SUBJECT AT THE BEGINNING OF THE SENTENCE:

> **An experienced pilot was at the controls at the time of the crash.**

SUBJECT AT THE END OF THE SENTENCE:

> **At the controls at the time of the crash was an experienced pilot.**

SUBJECT WITHIN THE SENTENCE:

> **At the time of the crash, an experienced pilot was at the controls.**

Finding the Subject

A sure way to find the subject is to answer one or the other of these questions:

a. About whom or about what is the sentence saying or asking something?

b. Who or what is doing, or has done, or will do something?

Question 1: What is the subject of the following sentence?

The score at the end of the quarter was 12–12.

Procedure: Ask yourself: "About what is the sentence saying something?"

Obviously, The score at the end of the quarter.

Answer: The subject is The score at the end of the quarter.

(The subject tells *about what* the sentence is saying something.)

Question 2: What is the subject of the following sentence?

The members of the orchestra tuned their instruments.

Procedure: Ask yourself: "Who did something?"

Answer: The subject is The members of the orchestra.

(The subject tells *who* did something.)

Question 3: What is the subject of the following?

Wait outside, please.

Procedure: Ask yourself: "Who is to wait outside?"

Answer: The subject is You (understood).

(You) wait outside, please.

Reminder: In an imperative sentence (a sentence expressing a command or making a request), the subject *You* is not expressed but understood.

Question 4: What is the subject of the following?

Is the door to the basement locked?

Procedure: Ask yourself: "Is what locked?"

Answer: The subject is the door to the basement.

(The subject tells *about what* the sentence is asking something.)

EXERCISE 1. Write the subject in the space provided.

Sample:

The apples in the fruit bowl were all sour.

The apples in the fruit bowl
_____

1. The next performance is at 9:15 P.M.
_____

2. An old jeep rolled to a stop by the side of the road.
_____

3. Did Philip come alone?
_____

4. Next to the hardware store is a furniture shop.
_____

5. Will your father drive us to the game?
_____

6. Give me your new address.
_____

7. Is the noise from the next room bothering you?
_____

8. The woman on the witness stand seemed a bit nervous.
_____

9. Our math teacher coaches the bowling team.
_____

10. The bowling team is coached by our math teacher.
_____

Simple Subject and Complete Subject

When a subject consists of more than one word, the main word in that subject is called the *simple subject*.

The seats on the bus are very comfortable.

SIMPLE SUBJECT: seats

The simple subject and the words that describe it are together known as the *complete subject*.

> COMPLETE SUBJECT: The seats on the bus

Question: Does a simple subject ever consist of more than one word?

Answer: Yes, especially if it is a name. For example:

> The late **Amelia Earhart** was a pioneer in aviation.
>
> > COMPLETE SUBJECT: The late Amelia Earhart
> > SIMPLE SUBJECT: Amelia Earhart
>
> The beautiful *Venus de Milo* is the work of an unknown sculptor.
>
> > COMPLETE SUBJECT: The beautiful *Venus de Milo*
> > SIMPLE SUBJECT: *Venus de Milo*

EXERCISE 2.   Write the complete subject in the **C.S.** space and the simple subject in the **S.S.** space.

Sample:

The first reporters on the scene did not get all the facts.

C.S. *The first reporters on the scene*   S.S. *reporters*

Hint: You can be sure that you have correctly chosen the simple subject if you can prove to yourself that it can not be omitted. If *The*, *first*, and *on the scene* were omitted from the C.S., above, the sentence would still make sense. But if *reporters* were omitted, the sentence would not make sense. This proves that *reporters* is the simple subject.

1. A player in a Wildcat uniform limped off the field.

   C.S. _____   S.S. _____

2. Light snow began to fall in the late afternoon.

   C.S. _____   S.S. _____

3. The famous *Mona Lisa* is a painting by Leonardo da Vinci.

   C.S. _____   S.S. _____

4. Did a letter from your sister come this morning?

   C.S. _____   S.S. _____

5. The small bar of chocolate is quite expensive.

   C.S. _____   S.S. _____

6. Farther up on the hill is a house with white shutters.

C.S. _____ S.S. _____

7. The bus to the railroad station is not running.

C.S. _____ S.S. _____

8. Asleep in the crib was a six-month-old infant.

C.S. _____ S.S. _____

9. My older brother is graduating in June.

C.S. _____ S.S. _____

10. The dust under the bed was quite thick.

C.S. _____ S.S. _____

lesson 5 The Predicate

Before talking about the *predicate*, let us review the *subject*.

The *subject* is the part of the sentence about which something is told or asked.

Prices are higher.
<u>subject</u>

Question: What is the *predicate*?

Answer: **The *predicate* is the part of the sentence that tells or asks something about the subject.**

Prices <u>are higher</u>.
<u>predicate</u>

Note how easily you can find the subject and the predicate of a sentence by asking two simple questions:

SENTENCE: **Prices are higher.**
QUESTION 1: About what is the sentence telling something?
ANSWER: *Prices*.
The subject is <u>*Prices*</u>.

QUESTION 2: What is the sentence saying about *Prices?*
ANSWER: Prices *are higher*.
The predicate is <u>*are higher*</u>.

SENTENCE: **My sister Karen is waiting for us.**
QUESTION 1: About whom is the sentence telling something?
ANSWER: *My sister Karen*.
The subject is <u>*My sister Karen*</u>.

QUESTION 2: What is the sentence saying about *My sister Karen?*
ANSWER: My sister Karen *is waiting for us*.
The predicate is <u>*is waiting for us*</u>.

SENTENCE: **Was Andy angry?**
QUESTION 1: About whom is the sentence asking something?
ANSWER: *Andy*.
The subject is <u>*Andy*</u>.

QUESTION 2: What is the sentence asking about *Andy?*
ANSWER: *Was* Andy *angry?*
The predicate is <u>*Was angry*</u>.

Position of the Predicate

The predicate usually comes after the subject, but it can also appear in other positions.

PREDICATE AFTER THE SUBJECT:

<u>The parking field</u> <u>is next to the stadium.</u>
      S.   P.

PREDICATE BEFORE THE SUBJECT:

<u>Next to the stadium</u> <u>is the parking field.</u>
      P.   S.

PREDICATE PARTLY BEFORE AND PARTLY AFTER THE SUBJECT:

<u>Is</u> <u>the parking field</u> <u>next to the stadium?</u>
 P.   S.   P.

EXERCISE 1. First draw a single line under the complete subject of the sentence. Then, above the double line at the right, write the predicate.

Samples:

SUBJECT	PREDICATE
The <u>temperature</u> dropped suddenly.	*dropped suddenly*
Has the <u>plane</u> landed?	*Has . . . landed*
Under the tree lay <u>many rotting apples.</u>	*Under the tree lay*

1. Rough <u>winds</u> battered the vessel. _____
2. <u>Chris</u> dances gracefully. _____
3. The <u>end</u> of the strike is not in sight. _____
4. Has the <u>patient</u> recovered from the flu? _____
5. Behind the wheel was my <u>sister Maria.</u> _____
6. How comfortable these new <u>seats</u> are! _____
7. Finally, the <u>suspect</u> surrendered to the police. _____
8. A <u>flock</u> of seagulls rested on the beach. _____
9. <u>Nothing</u> was missing. _____
10. Is more <u>time</u> needed? _____

EXERCISE 2. Complete the sentence by adding a suitable predicate.

Samples:

The apple _*was not ripe.*_____

A speck of dust _*flew into my eye.*_____

1. The onion soup _____

2. A dog _____

3. Your jacket _____

4. The shop on the corner _____

5. My cousin Aldo _____

6. Her new pen _____

7. The owner of the car _____

8. My desk _____

9. An old friend _____

10. His sister Julia _____

lesson 6 The Verb

The main word in the predicate is called the *verb*.

1. The temperature ***dropped*** rapidly.

   PREDICATE: dropped rapidly

   VERB: dropped

2. José often ***visits*** the art exhibits at the museum.

   PREDICATE: often visits the art exhibits at the museum

   VERB: visits

3. ***Have*** you any money?

   PREDICATE: Have any money

   VERB: Have

Without a verb, the predicate cannot tell or ask anything about the subject. See what happens if the verb is left out.

The temperature . . . rapidly.   (verb *dropped* omitted)

José often . . . the art exhibits at the museum.   (verb *visits* omitted)

. . . you any money?   (verb *Have* omitted)

Without verbs, the above sentences cannot convey any clear meaning.

Question: Does a verb ever consist of more than one word?

Answer: Yes, very often. A verb may consist of from one to four words:

SENTENCE	VERB
Have you any questions?	Have
Do you have any questions?	Do . . . have
We have been calling John all week.	have been calling
His phone may have been disconnected.	may have been disconnected

EXERCISE 1. Find the verb and write it in the blank space.

Samples:

Ben was at the door.   *was*

They must have been treated badly.   *must have been treated*

1. Mindy has many friends.   _____
2. The food is warming on the stove.   _____
3. Business has been very good.   _____
4. My headache has disappeared.   _____
5. I should have listened to you.   _____
6. He must have been pushed by someone.   _____
7. She has been told the truth.   _____
8. The pipe may have been leaking all night.   _____
9. We will try harder.   _____
10. Did the light bother you?   _____

EXERCISE 2. Write the *simple subject* in the **S.S.** space, the *predicate* in the **P.** space, and the *verb* in the **V.** space.

Samples:

The pond froze during the night.
S.S. *pond*
P. *froze during the night*
V. *froze*

Wash your hands.
S.S. *You* (understood)
P. *Wash your hands*
V. *Wash*

Did you hear the wind?
S.S. *you*
P. *Did hear the wind*
V. *Did hear*

1. The alarm awakened me at 7 A.M.
S.S. _____
P. _____
V. _____

2. Comb your hair.
S.S. _____
P. _____
V. _____

3. Have you seen my books anywhere?   S.S. _____

P. _____

_____

V. _____

4. My new boots are a bit too tight.   S.S. _____

P. _____

V. _____

5. The bus will come at any minute.   S.S. _____

P. _____

V. _____

6. Has it been coming on time lately?   S.S. _____

P. _____

_____

V. _____

7. I must have misplaced one of my gloves.   S.S. _____

P. _____

_____

V. _____

8. For some time, light rain has been falling.   S.S. _____

P. _____

_____

V. _____

9. It must have been raining since dawn.   S.S. _____

P. _____

_____

V. _____

10. In my pocket was the missing glove.   S.S. _____

P. _____

V. _____

11. The team has been winning most of its games.   S.S. _____

P. _____

_____

V. _____

12. You behaved magnificently.

S.S. _____

P. _____

V. _____

13. Our fuel bills have been increasing from year to year.

S.S. _____

P. _____

_____

V. _____

14. The weather has been interfering with the spring crops.

S.S. _____

P. _____

_____

V. _____

15. A mysterious explosion broke many windows.

S.S. _____

P. _____

V. _____

16. Did Anna win a place on the softball team?

S.S. _____

P. _____

_____

V. _____

17. Hold that line!

S.S. _____

P. _____

V. _____

18. Does your flashlight need fresh batteries?

S.S. _____

P. _____

V. _____

19. Someone must have taken my books by mistake.

S.S. _____

P. _____

_____

V. _____

20. Dan has been complaining about a leg pain.

S.S. _____

P. _____

_____

V. _____

lesson 7 Subject and Predicate in Formal and Informal English

I. Each sentence below is incomplete because a subject or a predicate is missing. Make up a suitable subject or predicate, whichever is lacking, and write it in the blank space.

Samples:

A stray dog _ran into the gym._____

_Our science teacher_____ likes to tell jokes.

_I_____ never saw her before.

1. Someone in the audience _____

2. _____ skidded on the ice.

3. The woman in the green dress _____

4. _____ haven't heard a word.

5. My older brother _____

6. _____ ate her breakfast in a hurry.

7. Ice cream _____

8. _____ must have been very upset.

9. Cigarettes _____

10. _____ has become very expensive.

11. The old car _____

12. _____ needs a haircut.

13. The line outside the theater _____

14. _____ found a quarter.

15. Basketball _____

II. In *informal* English, such as ordinary everyday conversation, we sometimes leave out the subject and part of the predicate. For example, we may say:

Heard the news?

If we were to express the same thought in *formal* English, we would probably say:

Have you heard the news?

Note that we have added two things:

(1) a subject (*you*), and
(2) the missing part of the predicate: *Have*.

How would you express the following thoughts in *formal* English?

Samples:

Need any help? *Do you need any help?*

Sorry to see you go. *I am sorry to see you go.*

Care for another hamburger? *Would you care for another hamburger?*

1. Like to go for a dip? _____
2. Feeling better? _____
3. Pleased to meet you. _____
4. Thirsty? _____
5. Been thinking of you. _____
6. Seen a good movie lately? _____
7. Glad you're here. _____
8. Finished your dinner? _____
9. Been meaning to call you. _____
10. Like to join us? _____
11. Delighted to see you. _____
12. Going anywhere tomorrow? _____
13. Ever been to the zoo? _____
14. Having trouble? _____
15. Good of you to come. _____

III. Read the following telephone conversation.

1. Jackie, Ted.
2. How are you, Ted?
3. Fine, Jackie. How are you?
4. Much better.
5. Saw your cousin Dolores yesterday.
6. Where?
7. Brenda's house. Doing anything?
8. Not right now.
9. Interested in a game of softball?
10. Who's playing?
11. Harvey, Manny, Alice, and some of her friends.
12. Will Rube be there?
13. Don't know yet. I'll call him.
14. Where are we playing?
15. Barrett Park. Coming?
16. What time?
17. In half an hour.
18. See you there in half an hour.

What changes would be necessary if the above conversation were rewritten in *formal* English? If a line requires no change, write "no change." If any change is needed, *rewrite the entire line*.

The answers for the first three lines are provided as samples.

1. Jackie, this is Ted.

2. no change

3. I am fine, Jackie. How are you?

4. _____

5. _____

6. _____

7. _____

8. _____

9. _____

10. _____

11. _____

12. _____

13. _____

14. _____

15. _____

16. _____

17. _____

18. _____

lesson 8 Compound Subjects

**A *compound subject* consists of two or more subjects
of the same verb connected by *and* or *or*.**

1. Gloria **_and_** Ralph joined our group.
   <u>compound subject</u>   <u>verb</u>

> *Gloria* is a subject of the verb *joined*.
> *Ralph* is also a subject of the verb *joined*.

These two subjects of the same verb, connected by *and*, give us the compound subject
Gloria and Ralph.

2. Nickels, dimes, **_or_** quarters may be deposited.
   <u>compound subject</u>   <u>verb</u>

> *Nickels* is a subject of the verb *may be deposited*.
> So, too, are *dimes* and *quarters*.

These three subjects of the same verb, connected by *or*, give us the compound subject *Nickels, dimes, or quarters*.

Composition Hint

Compound subjects enable us to express ourselves in fewer words and without
repetition. If there were no compound subjects, we would have to say:

> Nickels may be deposited. Dimes may be deposited.
> Quarters may be deposited.

EXERCISE 1. Enter the compound subject in the space at the right.

Samples:

Rain or snow is expected.   *Rain or snow*

Did Terry and Mel agree with you?   *Terry and Mel*

GRAMMAR   27

1. Rivers and streams overflowed. _____

2. Vermont and New Hampshire are next to each other. _____

3. Are onions, lettuce, and carrots on your shopping list? _____

4. Paula, Emil, or I will help with the decorations. _____

5. Handball and track are my favorite sports. _____

6. Susan and Rita were absent yesterday and today. _____

7. Pen and paper are in the middle drawer. _____

8. Saturday and Sunday, fog and mist made travel difficult. _____

9. Republicans and Democrats are blaming one another. _____

10. Does Bill Lopez or Maria Jones live near you? _____

EXERCISE 2. Express the following in fewer words by using a compound subject.

Samples:

Your battery may be causing the trouble.
Your bulb may be causing the trouble.

> *Your battery or bulb may be*
> *causing the trouble.*

Dresses are on sale.
Slacks are on sale.
Jackets are on sale.

> *Dresses, slacks, and jackets are*
> *on sale.*

> *Note:* **When there are more than two subjects in a compound subject, put a comma after each one, except the last:**
>
> Dresses, slacks, and jackets . . .

1. The House passed the bill.
   The Senate passed the bill. _____

2. Carmela may be the next class president.
   Rufus may be the next class president. _____

3. Prices have gone up.
   Wages have gone up.
   Taxes have gone up. _____

ENGLISH ALIVE

4. A table will be needed.
   Four chairs will be needed.

   _____

   _____

5. The kitchen should be repainted.
   The bathroom should be repainted.

   _____

   _____

6. Lisa will be there.
   Lester will be there.
   Marie will be there.

   _____

   _____

7. Eggs are cheaper.
   Potatoes are cheaper.

   _____

   _____

8. Ruth could have scored the winning run.
   Alex could have scored the winning run.

   _____

   _____

9. Fresh air is good for us.
   Exercise is good for us.

   _____

   _____

10. Towels are in the linen closet.
    Washcloths are in the linen closet.

    _____

    _____

EXERCISE 3. Complete each sentence below by adding a compound subject.

Samples:

_____ *Friday and Saturday* _____ are the busiest shopping days of the week.

Did _____ *Jennifer or Lou* _____ tell you about my accident?

1. _____ are the coldest months of the year.

2. _____ will probably be chosen captain.

3. In yesterday's game, _____ did most of the scoring.

4. _____ can be bought in a stationery store.

5. _____ had birthdays recently.

6. Saturday and Sunday, _____ will be visiting their relatives.

7. _____ broadcast the latest weather reports.

8. Would _____ like to come to our picnic?

9. _____ are in the refrigerator.

10. Did _____ cross the finish line first?

lesson 9 Compound Verbs

A *compound verb* consists of two or more verbs of the same subject connected by *and*, *or*, or *but*.

The <u>runner</u> <u>stumbled *and* fell</u>.
       S.   compound verb

The verb *stumbled* tells what the subject *runner* did.
The verb *fell*, too, tells what the subject *runner* did.

These two verbs of the same subject, connected by *and*, give us the compound verb *stumbled and fell*.

Here are further examples of compound verbs:

The <u>wind</u> <u>moaned, whistled, *and* howled</u> all night.
       S.   compound verb

In the evening <u>I</u> often <u>read *or* watch</u> television.
        S.   compound verb

The old <u>car</u> <u>runs *but* uses</u> a great deal of oil.
       S.   compound verb

Question: May a sentence have both a compound subject and a compound verb?

Answer: Yes. Here is an example:

<u>Cindy *and* Luke</u> <u>sang *and* danced</u>.
compound subject   compound verb

Composition Hint

A common error in writing is unnecessary repetition of the subject.

> *I* parked the car. *I* shut off the engine. *I* put the key in my pocket.   (Three *I*'s.)

With a compound verb, we can avoid such repetition.

> *I* parked the car, shut off the engine, and put the key in my pocket.   (One *I*.)

EXERCISE 1. Do away with the repetition of the subject by using a compound verb.

Examples:

She jogs.
She swims.
She plays tennis.

She jogs, swims, and plays tennis.

We tried.
We did not succeed.

We tried but did not succeed.

> *Note:* When a compound verb consists of more than two parts, put a comma after each part, except the last:
>
> jogs, swims, and plays . . .

1. Fire endangers life.
   Fire destroys property.

2. I went in.
   I took one look.
   I left.

3. A true friend cares about you.
   A true friend shares your troubles.

4. They have money.
   They do not know how to spend it.

5. Should we leave?
   Should we wait a bit longer?

6. We closed the windows.
   We turned off the lights.
   We locked the door.

7. A good book holds your interest.
   A good book improves your mind.

8. He ordered a cheese sandwich.
   He left it untouched.

9. The lungs provide the blood with oxygen.
   The lungs remove carbon dioxide.

10. She borrowed my notes.
    She failed to return them.

Read the following passage:

[1]James and Benjamin Franklin were brothers. [2]They lived and worked in Boston in colonial times. [3]James, the older, operated a printing shop. [4]He employed Benjamin and taught him the printing trade. [5]Often, however, they quarreled and came to blows. [6]Finally, in 1723, Benjamin ran away.

[7]Benjamin arrived in Philadelphia, tired and hungry. [8]He saw a boy eating bread and engaged him in a conversation. [9]The boy gave Benjamin directions to a baker's shop. [10]Benjamin went there, ordered three pennies' worth of bread, and received three enormous loaves. [11]Their size astounded him. [12]Evidently, bread was much cheaper in Philadelphia than in Boston.

[13]Eating one loaf, Benjamin walked the streets of Philadelphia with another loaf under each arm. [14]He must have looked ridiculous. [15]Deborah Read saw him and laughed. [16]Seven years later, Deborah and Benjamin would become man and wife.

[17]Benjamin filled himself on the one loaf and gave the remaining two to a woman and her child. [18]Feeling thirsty, he went down to the wharf for a drink of river water. [19]Philadelphia must have been free of pollution in those days. [20]What person in his right mind would drink water straight from a river today?

EXERCISE 2. Below, write the subject and the verb of each sentence in the passage you have just read. *Caution:* some of the subjects are compound, and some of the verbs are compound. The subject and the verb of the first two sentences have been filled in for you as samples.

	SUBJECT	VERB
1.	*James and Benjamin Franklin*	*were*
2.	*They*	*lived and worked*
3.		
4.		
5.		
6.		
7.		
8.		
9.		
10.		
11.		
12.		

13. _____ _____

14. _____ _____

15. _____ _____

16. _____ _____

17. _____ _____

18. _____ _____

19. _____ _____

20. _____ _____

lesson 10 Nouns

In a sentence, a word may play one of eight parts. It may be either

1. a noun,
2. a pronoun,
3. a verb,
4. an adjective,

5. an adverb,
6. a preposition,
7. a conjunction, or
8. an interjection.

These eight parts are known as the *parts of speech*.

We use the parts of speech to build sentences. For example, if we put together the noun *sunburn* and the verb *itches*, we can make the statement:

Sunburn itches.
N.   V.

If we wish, we can expand this statement by adding the adjective *my*,

My sunburn itches.
ADJ.   N.   V.

and the adverb *painfully*.

My sunburn itches *painfully*.
ADJ.   N.   V.   ADV.

If we should want to ask a question, we can begin with a verb. Here is a question made up of the verb *is*, the noun *sunburn*, and the adjective *painful*.

Is sunburn painful?
V.   N.   ADJ.

Of course, we can expand this question. For example, we can add the adverb *usually*.

Is sunburn *usually* painful?
V.   N.   ADV.   ADJ.

The system that our language uses to put parts of speech together into sentences is known as *grammar*.

In this lesson we shall study some grammar by learning about the first part of speech—the *noun*.

Nouns

> **Nouns are words that name persons, animals, places, or things.**

Question 1: How many nouns are there in the following sentence?

An old fisherman who had no luck hooked a huge fish that pulled his boat far out to sea.

Answer: Five.
(1) fisherman (a person)
(2) luck (a thing)
(3) fish (an animal)
(4) boat (a thing)
(5) sea (a place)

Note that nouns name things we can see and touch, like *boat*, as well as things we cannot see or touch, like *luck*.

Question 2: How many nouns does the following sentence contain?

Divers fish for pearls in the Gulf of Mexico.

Answer: Three.
(1) Divers (persons)
(2) pearls (things)
(3) Gulf of Mexico (a place)

Important: *Fish*, which was a noun in the earlier sentence, is not a noun here because *it does not name anything.* Here, *fish* is a *verb* (a word that expresses action).

Question 3: May a noun consist of more than one word?

Answer: Yes. *Gulf of Mexico* is one noun. **Nouns of more than one word are called *compound nouns*.** Here are further examples of compound nouns:

post office
living room
Atlantic Ocean
San Francisco
Grand Central Parkway
Mr. Applebaum
sister-in-law

EXERCISE 1. Look at the italicized word. If it is used as a noun, write **N.** in the space provided. If it is used as a verb, write **V.**

Samples:

a. We always *lock* the door.   _V._

b. Can you open the *lock?*   _N._

> **Explanation:** In sentence *a*, *lock* does not name anything. It expresses action. It is not a noun but a verb. In sentence *b*, *lock* names a thing. It is a noun.

1. a. Joyce *dresses* well. _____

    b. Joyce bought two *dresses.* _____

2. a. I ate three *slices* of pizza. _____

    b. This machine *slices* bread. _____

3. a. Many birds *fly* south for the winter. _____

    b. A *fly* buzzed past my ear. _____

4. a. You have a pleasing *smile.* _____

    b. *Smile* for the camera. _____

5. a. Oatmeal *cooks* in a few minutes. _____

    b. Good *cooks* make delicious meals. _____

6. a. What a fine *throw* you made! _____

    b. Pitchers *throw* curves and fast balls. _____

7. a. Luke did a fancy *dive.* _____

    b. *Dive* at your own risk. _____

8. a. Please *hand* me that book. _____

    b. Your *hand* is bleeding. _____

9. a. Did you hear a *knock?* _____

    b. *Knock* on the door. _____

10. a. *Look* at this mess! _____

    b. Her room has a neat *look.* _____

EXERCISE 2. List all the nouns in the following sentences.

Samples:

The driver stopped at the post office to mail a package.
NOUNS: *driver, post office, package*

My soul has grown deep like the rivers. (Langston Hughes)
NOUNS: *soul, rivers*

A man was starving in Capri. (Edna St. Vincent Millay)
NOUNS: *man, Capri*

1. Fog forced the airport to close.

2. The fleet has left the Indian Ocean.

3. Mrs. Thorpe has invited two sisters and a brother-in-law.

4. Mr. Jones of the Manor Farm had locked the hen-houses for the night, but was too drunk to remember to shut the popholes. (George Orwell)

5. In March, blackbirds return and trees begin to send out new leaves.

6. Joyce was on the driveway washing her car with a pail of water and some old rags.

7. George went back through the swinging-door into the kitchen and untied Nick and the cook. (Ernest Hemingway)

8. New York City has a larger population than San Francisco.

9. Have some more carrots and beans.

10. Did the team show any signs of improvement in the second quarter?

lesson 11 Common Nouns and Proper Nouns

Compare the following sentences:

1. We are approaching a lake.
2. We are approaching Lake Michigan.

Question: Why doesn't *lake* in sentence 1 begin with a capital (large) letter, like *Lake Michigan* in sentence 2?

Answer: In sentence 1, *lake* can refer to *any lake*. For this reason we call *lake* a *common noun*, and we do not capitalize it.

In sentence 2, *Lake Michigan* refers to a *particular lake*. Therefore, we call it a *proper noun*, and we capitalize it.

Question: What is a *proper noun?*

Answer: **A *proper noun* refers to *one particular person*, *animal*, *place*, *or thing***—like *Lake Michigan* in sentence 2, above.

A proper noun is *always capitalized.*

Question: What is a *common noun?*

Answer: **A *common noun* refers to *no particular person*, *animal*, *place*, *or thing*, but to any one at all**—like *lake* in sentence 1.

A common noun is *not* capitalized.

Compare the following sentences:

The office was closed because it was a **holiday.**
<u>common noun</u>

(*Holiday* is not capitalized because it is a *common noun*—it refers to *no holiday in particular.*)

The office was closed because it was **Thanksgiving.**
proper noun

(*Thanksgiving* is capitalized because it is a *proper noun*—it refers to *one particular holiday.*)

Here are some further examples of common nouns and proper nouns.

COMMON NOUNS	PROPER NOUNS
(*not* capitalized)	(*always* capitalized)
day (any day)	Monday
month (any month)	April
man (any man)	Wilbur Wright
woman (any woman)	Marian Anderson
bridge (any bridge)	Golden Gate Bridge
ocean (any ocean)	Pacific Ocean
dog (any dog)	Fido
event (any event)	World War II
magazine (any magazine)	*Newsweek*
institution (any institution)	Congress
monument (any monument)	Washington Monument
language (any language)	Spanish
club (any club)	Science Club
boy (any boy)	Jim
girl (any girl)	Nina

EXERCISE 1. List the common and proper nouns in the following sentences.

Samples:

The Brooklyn Bridge is the oldest bridge over the East River.

COMMON NOUNS: _*bridge*_

PROPER NOUNS: _*Brooklyn Bridge, East River*_

Heavy snow fell in the mountains over the weekend.

COMMON NOUNS: _*snow, mountains, weekend*_

PROPER NOUNS: _*none*_

1. Diane opened the door and let the cat out.

    COMMON NOUNS: _____

    PROPER NOUNS: _____

2. George Washington and Abraham Lincoln were born in February.

    COMMON NOUNS: _____

    PROPER NOUNS: _____

3. Call Frank from the airport as soon as the plane lands in Dallas.

    COMMON NOUNS: _____

    PROPER NOUNS: _____

4. Ken borrowed an eraser and a pencil from Amy.

COMMON NOUNS: _____

PROPER NOUNS: _____

5. The *Washington Post* reported that legislation has been introduced to reduce taxes.

COMMON NOUNS: _____

PROPER NOUNS: _____

6. Traffic is heavy in both directions on the Triboro Bridge and the Grand Central Parkway.

COMMON NOUNS: _____

PROPER NOUNS: _____

7. The whole town is talking about the coming game with Detroit.

COMMON NOUNS: _____

PROPER NOUNS: _____

8. Will the package reach Audrey before Christmas?

COMMON NOUNS: _____

PROPER NOUNS: _____

9. What a wonderful catch Eli made on that last play!

COMMON NOUNS: _____

PROPER NOUNS: _____

10. Considerable attention has been given by the press to the pollution of our lakes and rivers.

COMMON NOUNS: _____

PROPER NOUNS: _____

11. We took Dolores to the Metropolitan Opera to see *La Traviata* by Verdi.

COMMON NOUNS: _____

PROPER NOUNS: _____

12. Rice University and Baylor College of Medicine are both in Houston.

COMMON NOUNS: _____

PROPER NOUNS: _____

EXERCISE 2. Rewrite each sentence, changing the italicized common noun to a proper noun.

Samples:

The bus left the *school* on time.

*The bus left **Central High School** on time.*

An *ocean* is a vast body of water.

*The **Pacific Ocean** is a vast body of water.*

1. A *girl* was named captain.

2. We will meet outside the *theater*.

3. I saw an accident on the *street*.

4. Tomorrow is a *holiday*.

5. A *boy* asked a question.

6. When are you returning to the *city?*

7. Dad was reading the *newspaper*.

8. Does the *park* have handball courts?

9. We are four miles from the *river*.

10. I was talking to a *neighbor*.

Read the following passage:

"A Piece of Pie," an entertaining story by Damon Runyon, describes an eating contest in Mindy's Restaurant on Broadway. The contestants are Joel Duffle of Boston and Violette Shumberger of New York.

The Bostonian quickly takes the lead in the first course, consisting of two quarts of ripe olives, twelve bunches of celery, and four pounds of shelled nuts. However, by the time the main dish—an enormous turkey—is served, Violette has caught up with her opponent.

For dessert, the waiters carry in a pumpkin pie as wide as the cover of a manhole. Guess what happens next.

EXERCISE 3. List all the proper nouns and all the common nouns in the passage. The first two answers have been filled in as samples.

PROPER NOUNS

1. *"A Piece of Pie"*
2. _____
3. _____
4. _____
5. _____
6. _____
7. _____
8. _____
9. _____
10. _____

COMMON NOUNS

1. *story*
2. _____
3. _____
4. _____
5. _____
6. _____
7. _____
8. _____
9. _____
10. _____
11. _____
12. _____
13. _____
14. _____
15. _____
16. _____
17. _____
18. _____
19. _____
20. _____

lesson 12 Forming the Plural of Nouns (Part I)

Singular and Plural

Nouns have a *singular* form and a *plural* form.

The *singular* is the form that means *only one*:

boy, girl, soda, hamburger, etc.

The *plural* is the form that means *more than one*:

boys, girls, sodas, hamburgers, etc.

EXERCISE 1. Write the form indicated.

Samples:

the plural of *window* _____windows_____

the singular of *kittens* _____kitten_____

1. the plural of *wall* _____

2. the singular of *chairs* _____

3. the plural of *passenger* _____

4. the singular of *rainbows* _____

5. the plural of *elephant* _____

6. the singular of *gloves* _____

7. the plural of *bandage* _____

8. the singular of *armchairs* _____

9. the plural of *tree* _____

10. the singular of *vegetables* _____

Now that we have become familiar with the terms *singular* and *plural*, let us examine the singular and plural of a few more nouns.

SINGULAR (only one)	PLURAL (more than one)
1. hat	hats
2. box	boxes
3. leaf	leaves
4. foot	feet

In line 1, above, the plural is formed in a regular way: only *s* is added to form the plural of *hat*.

But in line 2, *es* is added to form the plural of *box*.

In line 3, you will notice, two changes are required to form the plural of *leaf*: first, the *f* is changed to *v*; then, *es* is added.

And in line 4, neither *s* nor *es* is added. Instead, there is a change inside the word: *oo* becomes *ee*.

From the above examples, you can see that there is no single rule for forming the plural of nouns; there are several.

This lesson will explain some of these rules. If you memorize them and do the exercises carefully, you will be well on your way to spelling plurals correctly.

Rule 1. For most nouns:

Add *s* to the singular to form the plural.

SINGULAR			PLURAL
ear	+ s	=	ears
chair	+ s	=	chairs
table	+ s	=	tables
face	+ s	=	faces

Question: How can I form the plural of words like *class* or *dish*? Can I just add *s*?

Answer: No, because [classs] and [dishs] would be hard to pronounce. We must do something else. This brings us to Rule 2.

Rule 2. For nouns ending in *s, sh, ch,* or *x:*

Add *es* to form the plural.

NOUNS ENDING IN *s:*	class	+ es	=	classes
	dress	+ es	=	dresses
NOUNS ENDING IN *sh:*	dish	+ es	=	dishes
	wish	+ es	=	wishes
NOUNS ENDING IN *ch:*	bench	+ es	=	benches
	lunch	+ es	=	lunches
NOUNS ENDING IN *x:*	box	+ es	=	boxes
	tax	+ es	=	taxes

Exceptions: The following nouns add neither *s* nor *es*, but form their plurals in an irregular way:

man	men
woman	women
child	children
foot	feet
tooth	teeth
louse	lice
mouse	mice
goose	geese
ox	oxen

EXERCISE 2. Write the plural of the following nouns.

Samples:

hand   *hands*

wish   *wishes*

foot   *feet*

1. land _____
2. apple _____
3. man _____
4. price _____
5. ox _____
6. fee _____
7. wax _____
8. child _____
9. glass _____
10. louse _____

11. lamp _____
12. woman _____
13. annex _____
14. quart _____
15. eyelash _____
16. mouse _____
17. brush _____
18. goose _____
19. radish _____
20. genius _____

EXERCISE 3. Make the following nouns singular.

Sample:

grandchildren   *grandchild*

1. houses _____
2. lamps _____
3. gentlemen _____
4. addresses _____
5. congresswomen _____

6. flowers _____
7. circuses _____
8. porches _____
9. brushes _____
10. foxes _____

Rule 3. For most nouns ending in *f:*

Add *s* to form the plural.

$$belief + \underline{s} = beliefs$$
$$chief + \underline{s} = chiefs$$
$$grief + \underline{s} = griefs$$
$$roof + \underline{s} = roofs$$
$$staff + \underline{s} = staffs$$

Exceptions: The following nouns ending in *f* change *f* to *v* and add *es:*

leaf	leaves
loaf	loaves
half	halves
self	selves
shelf	shelves
thief	thieves
wolf	wolves

But not in a name:

Mr. Wolf	The Wolfs

Rule 4. For three nouns ending in *fe—knife, life,* and *wife:*

Change *f* to *v* and add *s* to form the plural.

knife	knives
life	lives
wife	wives

EXERCISE 4.   In each sentence below, a plural noun has some letters missing. Fill in the missing letters. Then spell the whole word in the space at the right.

Sample:

I cut the apple into two equal h *a l v e* s.   *halves*

1. One loaf may not be enough. Buy two l_ _ _ _s.   _____

2. The mayor spoke with the c_ _ _ _ _s of the police, fire, and sanitation departments.   _____

3. How many s_ _ _ _ _s does your bookcase have?   _____

4. The husbands and their w_ _ _ _s sat opposite each other.   _____

5. You will see a television antenna on most of the r_ _ _s.   _____

6. A cat is reputed to have nine l_ _ _s.   _____

7. Foxes and w_ _ _ _s resemble dogs. _____

8. Do you still believe in fairness and honesty, or have you given up on these b_ _ _ _ _s? _____

9. Mrs. Wolf was on the telephone while the rest of the W_ _ _s were watching TV. _____

10. Several t_ _ _ _ _s and pickpockets were taken into custody. _____

EXERCISE 5.   Make the following nouns singular.

Sample:

knives   *knife* _____

1. cliffs   _____
2. leaves   _____
3. staffs   _____
4. lives   _____
5. proofs   _____

6. griefs   _____
7. thieves   _____
8. puffs   _____
9. selves   _____
10. churches   _____

lesson 13 Forming the Plural of Nouns (Part II)

This lesson requires us to know what is meant by *vowels* and *consonants*. Therefore, let us review them.

Vowels and Consonants

The *vowels* are *a, e, i, o,* and *u*. All of the other letters of the alphabet are *consonants*.

EXERCISE 1. Each of the following words ends in *y*. Look at the letter before *y*. If it is a vowel, write **V**. If it is a consonant, write **C**.

Samples:

way   <u>*V.*</u>   (*a* is a *vowel*)

lady   <u>*C.*</u>   (*d* is a *consonant*)

1. key	_____		6. enemy	_____
2. spy	_____		7. toy	_____
3. joy	_____		8. factory	_____
4. baby	_____		9. journey	_____
5. turkey	_____		10. company	_____

Plural of Nouns Ending in *Y*

To form the plural of a noun ending in *y*—like *way* or *lady*—first ask yourself:

Is the letter before *y* a *vowel* or a *consonant?*

Then follow Rule 5 or 6.

Rule 5. If the letter before *y* is a *vowel*, add *s* to form the plural.

SINGULAR   PLURAL

way + <u>s</u> = ways
key + <u>s</u> = keys
toy + <u>s</u> = toys

Rule 6. If the letter before *y* is a *consonant*, change the *y* to *i* and add *es*.

SINGULAR   PLURAL

lady   ladi<u>es</u>
enemy   enemi<u>es</u>
spy   spi<u>es</u>

EXERCISE 2. Make the following nouns plural.

Samples:

journey   *journeys*

factory   *factories*

1. valley
2. baby
3. party
4. highway
5. company
6. joy
7. bakery
8. monkey
9. pharmacy
10. chimney

EXERCISE 3. Make the following nouns singular.

Samples:

pennies   *penny*

turkeys   *turkey*

1. puppies
2. holidays

3. anniversaries   _____

4. juries   _____

5. strawberries   _____

6. attorneys   _____

7. ferries   _____

8. bluejays   _____

9. jellies   _____

10. envoys   _____

Plural of Nouns Ending in *O*

Rule 7. **If a noun ends in a *vowel plus o*, add *s* to form the plural.**

ENDING	SINGULAR	PLURAL
VOWEL e + *o*	stereo + s =	stereos
VOWEL i + *o*	radio + s =	radios

Rule 8. **If a noun ends in a *consonant plus o*, add *s* in most cases.**

auto   + s = autos
two   + s = twos
alto   + s = altos
piano   + s = pianos
solo   + s = solos
soprano + s = sopranos

Exceptions: Add *es* to the following nouns:

potato   + es = potatoes
tomato + es = tomatoes
echo   + es = echoes
veto   + es = vetoes

EXERCISE 4. Make the following nouns plural.

Sample:

patio   *patios* _____

1. studio   _____

2. rodeo   _____

3. potato   _____

4. portfolio   _____

5. tomato   _____

6. ratio   _____

7. veto   _____

8. trio   _____

9. echo   _____

10. piano   _____

EXERCISE 5. In each sentence below, a plural noun has some letters missing. Fill in the missing letters. Then spell the whole word in the space at the right.

Sample:

Violins, flutes, and p*i a n o*s are musical instruments.

                                   pianos _____

1. They spend more time watching TV than listening to their r_ _ _ _s.

           _____

2. Quartets have four performers, but t_ _ _s have three.

           _____

3. S_ _ _s have only one.

           _____

4. Some a_ _ _ _s run on diesel fuel.

           _____

5. Do you like french fried p_ _ _ _ _ _s?

           _____

6. Chemists perform experiments in laboratories, but painters and sculptors work in s_ _ _ _ _ _s.

           _____

7. Vitamin C is present in oranges, grapefruits, and t_ _ _ _ _ _ _s.

           _____

8. Congress voted to override two of the President's v_ _ _ _s.

           _____

9. The singers in the chorus are mainly altos and s_ _ _ _ _ _s.

           _____

10. Any sounds we make while passing through a tunnel or cave hit the walls and bounce back as e_ _ _ _s.

           _____

lesson 14 Reviewing the Plural of Nouns

SUMMARY OF THE RULES

When to add *S*.

A. To most nouns: book—books. (See Rule 1, page 44.)

A–X.   *Exceptions to A:*

man—men	foot—feet	mouse—mice
woman—women	tooth—teeth	goose—geese
child—children	louse—lice	ox—oxen

(See Rule 2 Exceptions, page 45.)

B. To most nouns ending in *f:* belief—beliefs. (See Rule 3, page 46.)

B–X.   *Exceptions to B:*

leaf—leaves	shelf—shelves
loaf—loaves	thief—thieves
half—halves	wolf—wolves
self—selves	

C. To nouns ending in a *vowel + y:* way—ways. (See Rule 5, page 49.)

D. To nouns ending in a *vowel + o:* radio—radios. (See Rule 7, page 50.)

E. To most nouns ending in a *consonant + o:* auto—autos. (See Rule 8, page 50.)

When to add *ES*.

E–X.   *Exceptions to E:*

potato + es = potatoes	echo + es = echoes
tomato + es = tomatoes	veto + es = vetoes

F. To nouns ending in *s:*   class   + es = classes
            sh: wish   + es = wishes
            ch: bench + es = benches
        or *x:* box   + es = boxes

(See Rule 2, page 44.)

When to change Y to I and add ES.

> G. When a noun ends in a *consonant + y:* lady—ladies. (See Rule 6, page 49.)

When to change F to V and add S.

> H. In the following three nouns ending in *fe* and their compounds:
>
> > knife—knives
> > life—lives
> > wife—wives
> > penknife—penknives
> > housewife—housewives
> > (See Rule 4, page 46.)

EXERCISE. For each singular noun below, write
  (a) the plural, and
  (b) the *letter* of the rule for forming that plural. Take your rule letters from the preceding four boxes.

Samples:

SINGULAR	PLURAL	RULE LETTER
notebook	*notebooks*	*A*
penknife	*penknives*	*H*
tax	*taxes*	*F*
baby	*babies*	*G*
photo	*photos*	*E*
potato	*potatoes*	*E-X*
cliff	*cliffs*	*B*
alley	*alleys*	*C*
loaf	*loaves*	*B-X*
ox	*oxen*	*A-X*
1. pencil		
2. leaf		
3. proof		
4. highway		
5. child		

6. tomato _____ _____

7. portfolio _____ _____

8. mountain _____ _____

9. louse _____ _____

10. piano _____ _____

11. class _____ _____

12. sheriff _____ _____

13. housewife _____ _____

14. tree _____ _____

15. torch _____ _____

16. thief _____ _____

17. echo _____ _____

18. tooth _____ _____

19. party _____ _____

20. tariff _____ _____

21. alto _____ _____

22. cloud _____ _____

23. shelf _____ _____

24. landlady _____ _____

25. woman _____ _____

26. branch _____ _____

27. studio _____ _____

28. jackknife _____ _____

29. six _____ _____

30. alloy _____ _____

31. handbag _____ _____

32. jury _____ _____

33. dash _____ _____

34. stepchild _____ _____

35. rodeo _____ _____

36. life _____ _____

37. soprano _____ _____

38. pie _____ _____

39. monkey _____ _____

40. witch _____ _____

lesson 15 Forming Possessive Nouns

Question: If you were running for office, which would be more important to you—

        (*a*) your *friend's* support, or

        (*b*) your *friends'* support?

Answer: (*b*).

Explanation: *Friend's* means "of a friend."

If you have your *friend's* support, you have the support of *only one friend*.

Friends' means "of friends."

If you have your *friends'* support, you have the support of *more than one friend*.

Question: What is a *possessive noun?*

Answer: **A *possessive noun* is a noun that shows possession or ownership.**

A *possessive noun* always contains an *apostrophe* ['].

    We have already met two possessive nouns—*friend's* and *friends'*. Here are some further examples of possessive nouns:

1. *student's* money   The possessive noun *student's* shows that the money belongs to the student.

2. *students'* money   The possessive noun *students'* shows that the money belongs to the students.

3. *children's* money   The possessive noun *children's* shows that the money belongs to the children.

Question: Why does the apostrophe come before the *s* in examples 1 and 3, above, but after the *s* in example 2?

Answer: Over the centuries, English has developed a few rules for using the apostrophe to show possession. These rules can be summed up as follows:

Note that a possessive noun can help us express ourselves in fewer words. Instead of *money belonging to the children* (5 words), we can say *children's money* (2 words).

Let us now go over the above three rules with some further examples.

Rule 1. If the possessor is a SINGULAR NOUN, add an APOSTROPHE AND S.

the eyes of the *baby*	becomes the **baby's** eyes
the eraser that *Mary* owns	becomes **Mary's** eraser
the whiskers of the *cat*	becomes the **cat's** whiskers
the glove belonging to *Otis*	becomes **Otis's** glove
the novels by *Dickens*	becomes **Dickens's** novels

EXERCISE 1. Express each of the following phrases in fewer words.

Sample:

the name of the visitor   *the visitor's name* _____

1. the bark of the dog   _____

2. the books belonging to Frank   _____

3. the car that Iris owns   _____

4. the house where Joe lives   _____

5. the letter Gladys wrote   _____

Rule 2. If the possessor is a PLURAL NOUN ENDING IN S, add ONLY AN APOSTROPHE.

the hats belonging to the *girls*   becomes the **girls'** hats
the coats owned by the *students*   becomes the **students'** coats
the nests of *birds*   becomes the **birds'** nests

EXERCISE 2. Express in fewer words.

1. the mailboxes of neighbors   _____

2. tools used by carpenters   _____

3. the uniforms nurses wear   _____

4. the reasons the Senators gave   _____

5. the money belonging to the depositors   _____

Rule 3. If the possessor is a PLURAL NOUN *NOT* ENDING IN S, first write the plural; then add an APOSTROPHE AND S.

shoes worn by *men*   becomes **men's** shoes
suits for *women*   becomes **women's** suits
the faces of *people*   becomes **people's** faces

EXERCISE 3. Express in fewer words.

1. the names of the grandchildren   _____

2. the luggage belonging to the Englishmen   _____

3. the wages the men earned   _____

4. the protests of the townspeople   _____

5. the reasons given by the women   _____

EXERCISE 4. Write the correct possessive form of the noun in parentheses.

Sample:

My ___*brother's*___ name is Jack. (*brother*)

1. I borrowed my _____ science notes. (*friend*)

2. My _____ names are Lee, Lorraine, and Frieda. (*sisters*)

3. _____ father is an engineer. (*Phyllis*)

4. We hold our dances in the _____ gym. (*boys*)

5. How much were the _____ fees? (*lawyers*)

6. Where did you put _____ umbrella? (*Ellen*)

7. _____ house is near the athletic field. (*Lewis*)

8. There is a sale on _____ slacks. (*women*)

9. Did the manager listen to the _____ complaints? (*customers*)

10. A dictator has little regard for _____ wishes. (*people*)

11. The _____ names are Madame Vigny and Madame Strauss. (*Frenchwomen*)

12. Are you _____ sister? (*Dennis*)

13. I borrowed my _____ snow shovel. (*neighbor*)

14. Have the _____ passes been distributed? (*visitors*)

15. The British advance was slowed by the _____ resistance. (*Minutemen*)

Composition Hint _____

When you write a paragraph, or even a sentence, check to see if you can reduce the number of words you have used. Sometimes, a possessive noun can help. For example,

INSTEAD OF: the car that my brother has   (6 words),

WRITE: my ***brother's*** car   (3 words).
possessive
noun

EXERCISE 5.   Rewrite the following paragraph, using possessive nouns wherever possible. You should be able to reduce the number of words in the paragraph from 69 to 56.

The dog that Lois owns is huge but gentle. He tries to get the attention of her friends to show that he likes them. The parents of Lois, too, are fond of the dog. At first some neighbors were frightened by the size of the dog. They feared for the safety of their children. Now they no longer worry. By the way, the name of the dog is Tiny.

_____

_____

_____

_____

_____

_____

_____

_____

EXERCISE 6. As we have learned, a noun may have as many as four forms.

(1)	(2)	(3)	(4)
		POSSESSIVE	POSSESSIVE
SINGULAR	PLURAL	SINGULAR	PLURAL
student	students	student's	students'

On each line below, only one form of a noun is given. Write the other three forms of that noun.

	SINGULAR	PLURAL	POSSESSIVE SINGULAR	POSSESSIVE PLURAL
1.	girl	_____	_____	_____
2.	_____	children	_____	_____
3.	_____	_____	man's	_____
4.	_____	_____	_____	officers'
5.	voter	_____	_____	_____
6.	_____	teachers	_____	_____
7.	_____	_____	nurse's	_____
8.	_____	_____	_____	women's
9.	customer	_____	_____	_____
10.	_____	friends	_____	_____

lesson 16 Nouns as Direct Objects

Question 1: How is the noun *Amy* used in these two sentences?

    (1) *Amy* is our top scorer.

    (2) The crowd cheered *Amy*.

Answer: In the first sentence, the noun *Amy* is the *subject* of the verb *is*.

In the second sentence, the noun *Amy* is the *direct object* of the verb *cheered*.

Question 2: What is a *direct object*?

Answer: **A *direct object* is a word in the predicate that receives the action of the verb.**

In sentence 2, above, the noun *Amy* is the word in the predicate that receives the action of the verb *cheered*. Therefore, the noun *Amy* is the direct object of the verb *cheered*.

Important: There can be no direct object without an action verb.

Compare the noun *Amy* in the following sentences:

    (1) Our top scorer is *Amy*.

    (2) The crowd cheered *Amy*.

Sentence 1 cannot have a direct object because it has no action verb; *is* does not express action. *Amy*, in sentence 1, is not a direct object.

On the other hand, sentence 2 can have a direct object because it has an action verb; *cheered* expresses action. *Amy*, in sentence 2, receives the action of the verb *cheered* and is a direct object of that verb.

            The crowd cheered *Amy*.
            S.   V.   D.O.

Question: Are there other verbs, besides *is*, that do not express action?

Answer: Yes. Here are some of them:

am	will be	may be	have been
are	shall be	might be	has been
was	would be	can be	had been
were	should be	could be	will have been

In reality, all of the above verbs, including *is*, are forms of a single verb—the verb *be*.

Remember the following about *am, is, are, will be,* and all other forms of the verb *be:*

(1) **They do not express action.**
(2) **They cannot have a direct object.**

EXERCISE 1. In which sentence, *a* or *b*, is the italicized noun a direct object? Write the letters **D.O.** on the proper line.

Sample:

a. Agnes and Elmer are my *cousins*.   a. _____

b. I called my *cousins*.   b. ___D.O.___

1. a. Stephen Crane was a *reporter*.   a. _____
    b. The publisher dismissed the *reporter*.   b. _____

2. a. We will follow the *guide*.   a. _____
    b. Mona will be our *guide*.   b. _____

3. a. You may be an *artist* someday.   a. _____
    b. I watched the *artist* at work.   b. _____

4. a. Ginette plays two stringed *instruments*.   a. _____
    b. The violin, guitar, and cello are stringed *instruments*. b. _____

5. a. Rhoda has been *president* since April.   a. _____
    b. The members are blaming the *president*.   b. _____

6. a. One of the most challenging games is *chess*.   a. _____
    b. Two of my friends play *chess*.   b. _____

7. a. For years Dr. Kroll had been our *dentist*.   a. _____
    b. We have found a new *dentist*.   b. _____

8. *a.* The vegetables for today are peas and *squash*.   *a.* _____

    b. Hal had some buttered *squash*.   *b.* _____

9. *a.* Caroline drives a *Ford*.   *a.* _____

    b. This is a *Ford*.   *b.* _____

10. *a.* Mr. Reed is Jean's *teacher*.   *a.* _____

    b. The district has hired a new art *teacher*.   *b.* _____

Easy Procedure for Finding the Direct Object

To find the direct object, ask the question WHAT? or WHOM? right after the action verb.

Question 1:   What is the direct object in the following sentence?

                Caroline drives a Ford.

Procedure: Caroline drives a WHAT?

Answer: *Ford* is the direct object.

Question 2:   What is the direct object in the following?

                I watched the artist at work.

Procedure: I watched WHOM at work?

Answer: *Artist* is the direct object.

Note that a direct object may be *compound:* **it may consist of more than one word.** The following sentence has a compound direct object:

Heavy rain flooded the **streets and highways**.
       S.   V.   compound direct object

EXERCISE 2. In each sentence below, find the verb (**V.**), the subject (**S.**), and the direct object (**D.O.**).

Samples:

Water loosens the soil.   V.   *loosens* _____

                            S.   *Water* _____

                            D.O.   *soil* _____

The team has already left.   V.   *has left* _____

                            S.   *team* _____

                            D.O.   *none* _____

Cathy and Armando distributed the programs.	V.	*distributed*
	S.	*Cathy and Armando*
	D.O.	*programs*
Open and count the ballots.	V.	*Open and count*
	S.	*You* (understood)
	D.O.	*ballots*
Did Frank get a single and a triple?	V.	*did get*
	S.	*Frank*
	D.O.	*single and triple*

1. Squirrels like nuts.

V. _____

S. _____

D.O. _____

2. Iron rusts.

V. _____

S. _____

D.O. _____

3. The speaker's question surprised and amused the audience.

V. _____

S. _____

D.O. _____

4. Have some milk and cookies.

V. _____

S. _____

D.O. _____

5. The players and cheerleaders returned.

V. _____

S. _____

D.O. _____

6. Are the snow and ice melting?

V. _____

S. _____

D.O. _____

7. Seventeen members have paid their dues.

V. _____

S. _____

D.O. _____

8. Radio and television provide information and entertainment.

V. _____

S. _____

D.O. _____

9. Jonathan returned the books to the library.

V. _____

S. _____

D.O. _____

10. The motel provides soap and towels.

V. _____

S. _____

D.O. _____

lesson 17 Nouns as Indirect Objects

Question 1: How is the noun *Amy* used in the following sentence?

The crowd gave *Amy* a *cheer*.
S.   V.   ?   D.O.

Answer: *Amy* is the *indirect object* of the verb *gave*.

Explanation: **An *indirect object* is a word in the predicate that tells FOR WHOM or TO WHOM something was done, or is being done, or will be done.**

Note that there are two nouns after the action verb *gave: Amy* and *cheer*.

The noun *cheer* is the *direct object* of *gave* because it answers the question WHAT? (The crowd gave WHAT?)

The noun *Amy* tells FOR WHOM the crowd gave a cheer. Therefore, *Amy* is the *indirect object* of the verb *gave*.

The crowd gave *Amy* a *cheer*.
S.   V.   I.O.   D.O.

The above sentence shows that an action verb can have both a *direct object* and an *indirect object* in the same sentence.

Question 2: Which comes first in a sentence, the direct object or the indirect object?

Answer: The indirect object always comes before the direct object. Note these further examples:

A friend sent *Marilyn* a *card*.
I.O.   D.O.

(*Marilyn* is the indirect object because it tells TO WHOM a friend sent a card.)

Grandma is knitting *Bob* a *sweater*.
I.O.   D.O.

(*Bob* is the indirect object because it tells FOR WHOM Grandma is knitting a sweater.)

The firm pays its ***officers*** a *salary*.
               I.O.   D.O.

(*Officers* is the indirect object because it tells TO WHOM the firm pays a salary.)

EXERCISE 1. For each sentence, indicate the verb (**V.**), the subject (**S.**), the indirect object (**I.O.**), if any, and the direct object (**D.O.**), if any.

Samples:

Sunburn itches.	V.	*itches*
	S.	*Sunburn*
	I.O.	*none*
	D.O.	*none*

Ms. Jones will tell the truth.	V.	*will tell*
	S.	*Ms. Jones*
	I.O.	*none*
	D.O.	*truth*

Ms. Jones will tell the court the truth.	V.	*will tell*
	S.	*Ms. Jones*
	I.O.	*court*
	D.O.	*truth*

1. Prices fell.

   V. _____
   S. _____
   I.O. _____
   D.O. _____

2. The merchant offered a discount.

   V. _____
   S. _____
   I.O. _____
   D.O. _____

3. The merchant offered the customer a discount.

   V. _____
   S. _____
   I.O. _____
   D.O. _____

4. Did the judge grant the suspect bail?

V. _____

S. _____

I.O. _____

D.O. _____

5. The city will build the Giants a new stadium.

V. _____

S. _____

I.O. _____

D.O. _____

6. Rhoda showed the guard her pass.

V. _____

S. _____

I.O. _____

D.O. _____

7. Rosalie and Eric bought Dad a watch.

V. _____

S. _____

I.O. _____

D.O. _____

8. Gerald has made his parents a promise.

V. _____

S. _____

I.O. _____

D.O. _____

9. A passerby slipped and fell.

V. _____

S. _____

I.O. _____

D.O. _____

10. The directors have voted the president and vice-president a raise.

V. _____

S. _____

I.O. _____

D.O. _____

11. Carlotta made her sister-in-law a party.

V. _____

S. _____

I.O. _____

D.O. _____

EXERCISE 2. Rewrite the sentence, changing the italicized expression to an indirect object.

Sample:

Did you give the assignment *to Nick?*

Did you give Nick the assignment?

1. Fred sent a birthday card *to Nancy.*

2. Have you ever done a favor *for John?*

3. Phil is lending his science notes *to Madeline.*

4. Rose is making a blouse *for her sister.*

5. Give the tickets *to the usher.*

6. Who baked a cake *for Herman?*

7. Please cut a slice of melon *for Vera.*

8. Washington is giving emergency aid *to the stricken areas.*

9. I wrote a letter *to Marie.*

10. The salesclerk handed the change *to the customer.*

lesson 18 Pronouns and Their Antecedents

A *pronoun* is a word that takes the place of a noun.

Question 1:   How many pronouns are there in the following sentence?

Paul Steinbrenner promised Rosalie Amato that he would vote for her.

Answer: Two.

He is a *pronoun* taking the place of *Paul Steinbrenner*.
Her is a *pronoun* taking the place of *Rosalie Amato*.

Question 2:   What is an *antecedent?*

Answer: **An *antecedent* is the noun that a pronoun stands for.**

In the sentence above, the *antecedent* of the pronoun *he* is the noun *Paul Steinbrenner;* the *antecedent* of the pronoun *her* is the noun *Rosalie Amato*.

Question 3:   Why are pronouns important?

Answer: Pronouns make language more interesting because they help us express ourselves without repetition and in fewer words.

If there were no pronouns, we would have to say:

Paul Steinbrenner promised Rosalie Amato that Paul Steinbrenner would vote for Rosalie Amato.

EXERCISE 1.   In the blank space, use a pronoun that can take the place of the italicized antecedent.

Samples:

Joyce has a new *bicycle* but has not used _____*it*_____.

Did *the Browns* say that _____*they*_____ would come?

The gloves are *Karen's*. The muffler is not _____*hers*_____.

1. Let *the soup* cool before tasting _____.

2. There is *Bruce*. Speak to _____.

3. The magazine is *Tom's*, but the newspaper is not _____.

4. *Isabel* has nothing to write with. Lend _____ a pen.

5. *Gina* knows that _____ is the next speaker.

6. *Al and Tony* arrived, but there were no seats for _____.

7. *Joe* did not come because _____ has a cold.

8. If *the girls* win today, _____ have a chance for the championship.

9. Has anyone seen *Roy's* notebook? Is that one _____?

10. The stationery was *Ellen's*, and the handwriting was _____, too.

EXERCISE 2. Find the pronoun (**pron.**) and its antecedent (**anteced.**), and write them in the spaces at the right.

Samples:

Sandra said she does not agree.	pron.	*she*
	anteced.	*Sandra*
The Declaration of Independence is an important historical document. It was issued on July 4, 1776.	pron.	*It*
	anteced.	*Declaration of Independence*
Fritz and Joe got on base; both scored.	pron.	*both*
	anteced.	*Fritz and Joe*

1. The challenger knows that he cannot win.

    pron. _____

    anteced. _____

2. Friday was stormy. It was a miserable day.

    pron. _____

    anteced. _____

3. Ask Eric and Annabel if they can come.

    pron. _____

    anteced. _____

4. Not one motel had a vacancy; each was booked to capacity.

    pron. _____

    anteced. _____

5. Lori adores cats, but Wendy hates them.

    pron. _____

    anteced. _____

6. "We want a hit!" yelled the fans.

    pron. _____

    anteced. _____

7. Grace complained: "Ruth has not invited me."

    pron. _____

    anteced. _____

8. Mr. Walsh told the salesclerk: "I always pay cash."

    pron. _____

    anteced. _____

9. Pointing to the blouse, Liz asked the salesclerk, "How much is this?"

    pron. _____

    anteced. _____

10. The committee asks: "Help us make this town a better place to live in."

    pron. _____

    anteced. _____

Composition Hint

To avoid repeating a noun you have just mentioned, use a pronoun.

DO NOT WRITE: I know Texas well because Texas is my home state.

WRITE: I know Texas well because _it_ is my home state.

The pronoun *it* enables you to avoid repeating the noun *Texas*.

EXERCISE 3. What pronoun can you use to avoid repeating the italicized word or words? Write your answer in the space provided.

Sample:

We did not invite Grace, though *Grace* would have liked to come.   *she*

1. The ball came right into your hands, but you could not hold on to *the ball*.   _____

2. The jacket is Tony's and the sweater is *Tony's*, too.   _____

3. Jane and Audrey are our friends. We have nothing against *Jane and Audrey*.   _____

4. They looked for pistachio ice cream, but *pistachio ice cream* was not on the menu.   _____

5. Ask the conductor. *The conductor* will be only too glad to help you.   _____

lesson 19 Personal Pronouns

The personal pronouns are

I, you, he, she, it, we, they.

They are called **personal pronouns** because, except for *it*, they all refer to *persons*.

These pronouns are among the most troublesome words in our language.

Question: Why are the personal pronouns troublesome?

Answer: Most of these pronouns change in form, depending on the way they are used in a sentence. On the other hand, the nouns that these pronouns stand for do not change.

For example, take the noun *George*. We can use *George* either as a subject, a direct object, or an indirect object.

George can be a SUBJECT:

> *George* complained.
> S.   V.

George can be a DIRECT OBJECT:

> The noise bothered *George*.
> S.   V.   D.O.

George can be an INDIRECT OBJECT:

> The noise gave *George* a headache.
> S.   V.   I.O.   D.O.

Obviously, the noun *George* does not change in form, whether used as a subject, a direct object, or an indirect object.

But most pronouns change in form, depending on their use. For example, *he* can be used as a subject, but *not* as a direct object or an indirect object.

He can be a SUBJECT:

> *He* complained.
> S.   V.

For a DIRECT OBJECT, we must use *him:*

> The noise bothered *him*.
> S.   V.   D.O.

Also, for an INDIRECT OBJECT we must use *him:*

> The noise gave *him* a headache.
> S.   V.   I.O.   D.O.

THE DIFFERENT FORMS OF THE PERSONAL PRONOUNS

If we need a pronoun as a SUBJECT, we can use one of the following:

I	you	he	she	it	we	they

If we need a pronoun as a DIRECT OBJECT or an INDIRECT OBJECT, we can use one of the following:

me	you	him	her	it	us	them

If we need a pronoun TO SHOW POSSESSION, we can use one of the following:

my, mine	your, yours	his	her, hers	its	our, ours	their, theirs

Note: Only *you* and *it* have the same form for subject, direct object, and indirect object.

EXERCISE 1. Supply the missing pronoun.

Samples:

Ernest likes music. _____*He*_____ plays the guitar.

It was Jim. I recognized _____*him*_____.

This book must be Pedro's. It is definitely _____*his*_____.

1. Isabel and I are neighbors. _____ live on the same street.

2. Joyce asked if the package belongs to us, but I told her it is not _____.

3. Our dog suffered an injury. It hurt _____ leg.

4. Marie is related to Rose. _____ is Rose's cousin.

5. Mel and Abe are our friends. We like _____.

6. This may be Carmelita's purse. Ask her if it is _____.

7. Eleanor and I will come when you call _____.

8. Mr. and Mrs. Stern have just made the last mortgage payment. Now the house is all _____.

9. You ordered these tickets. Take them. They are _____.

10. I admit I am to blame. The fault is _____.

Pronouns in Combinations

Pronouns and nouns may be combined to form compound subjects, compound indirect objects, and compound direct objects.

Edna and I attended.   (COMPOUND SUBJECT)
compd. S.

Peter showed *Edna and me* the pictures.   (COMPOUND INDIRECT OBJECT)
compd. I.O.

The instructor chose *Edna and me*.   (COMPOUND DIRECT OBJECT)
compd. D.O.

Composition Hint

Make your writing more interesting and more effective by removing unnecessary words. Note how compound subjects, compound indirect objects, and compound direct objects can help.

DO NOT WRITE: My friends liked the movie. I liked the movie.

WRITE: *My friends and I* liked the movie.
compd. S.

DO NOT WRITE: You gave Iris the wrong directions. You gave us the wrong directions.

WRITE: You gave *Iris and us* the wrong directions.
compd. I.O.

DO NOT WRITE: She invited her cousin. She invited me.

WRITE: She invited *her cousin and me*.
compd. D.O.

EXERCISE 2. Rewrite each pair of sentences as one sentence, taking out the unnecessary words. Your new sentence should contain a compound subject, compound indirect object, or compound direct object.

Sample:

Andrea asked several questions. I asked several questions.

Andrea and I asked several questions.

1. My friend joined the bowling team. I joined the bowling team.

_____

2. Diane met my cousin at the game. Diane met me at the game.

_____

3. Bruce will attend the meeting. She will attend the meeting.

_____

4. We offered Bill a place on the committee. We offered her a place on the committee.

_____

5. Our opponents have had a good season. We have had a good season.

_____

6. They have known the Russos a long time. They have known us a long time.

_____

7. My sister saw the play. He saw the play.

_____

8. Frank gave Jack the wrong number. Frank gave me the wrong number.

_____

9. Charlotte heard the crash. I heard the crash.

_____

10. Millie sends Ted her best regards. Millie sends us her best regards.

_____

lesson 20 Pronouns in Contractions

Suppose a salesclerk is helping you choose a shirt. After you have made your decision, which of the following are you more likely to say?

1. **I will take this one.**

2. **I'll take this one.**

It is more likely that you will say:

I'll take this one.

In rapid everyday speech, we run together the personal pronoun *I* and its verb *will*. As a result, *will* loses its first two letters, *w* and *i*. The expression we are left with, *I'll*, is called a *contraction*.

Question: What is a *contraction*?

Answer: **A *contraction* is a combination of two words, with one or more letters omitted. An *apostrophe* ['] takes the place of the omitted letters.**

PRONOUN	+	VERB	=	CONTRACTION	LETTERS OMITTED
you	+	are	=	*you're*	*a*
she	+	will	=	*she'll*	*w i*
I	+	would	=	*I'd*	*w o u l*

Note that the first word in a contraction does not lose any letters—only the second word does. In the following contraction, the pronoun *us* loses a letter because it is the second word.

let + us = *let's*

EXERCISE 1. What letter or letters are omitted in the italicized contraction?

Sample:

She's here. _____*i*_____

1. *It'll* rain. _____
2. *I'll* wait. _____
3. *He's* tired. _____
4. *We'd* be delighted. _____
5. *They're* angry. _____

6. *Let's* try. _____
7. *We've* eaten. _____
8. *I'm* ready. _____
9. *She'll* help. _____
10. *You'd* be surprised. _____

Contractions are commonly used in conversation and in friendly letters and notes. Study the following contractions:

it	+ is	= *it's*	I	+ am	= *I'm*
they	+ will	= *they'll*	we	+ are	= *we're*
you	+ have	= *you've*	he	+ would	= *he'd*

EXERCISE 2. A contraction stands for two words. Write the two words for each italicized contraction below.

Sample:

He'll go. = ____*He will*____

1. *I've* paid. = _____
2. *You'd* laugh! = _____
3. *It'll* melt. = _____
4. *They've* left. = _____
5. *Let's* stop. = _____

6. *They're* clever. = _____
7. *We'll* follow. = _____
8. *He's* nervous. = _____
9. *She'd* win. = _____
10. *It's* a pity. = _____

EXERCISE 3. Write each of the following as a contraction.

Sample:

they will = ____*they'll*____

1. let us = _____
2. you have = _____
3. they are = _____
4. we will = _____
5. it is = _____
6. you would = _____

7. we have = _____
8. I am = _____
9. I have = _____
10. they would = _____
11. you are = _____
12. I would = _____

Caution: Do not confuse a contraction with a possessive pronoun.

A contraction *always* has an apostrophe:

you'll (you will); **it's** (it is), etc.

A possessive pronoun *never* has an apostrophe:

yours, his, hers, its, ours, theirs

CONTRACTIONS	POSSESSIVE PRONOUNS
(*Use apostrophe to replace omitted letters.*)	(*Do not use apostrophe.*)
It's (It is) raining.	*Its* fur is soft.
You're (You are) wrong.	*Your* friend is here.
They're (They are) here.	*Their* parents came.

EXERCISE 4. Write the choice that makes the sentence correct.

Samples:

The employees want (*they're, their*) pay.   _their_____

Note that in the above sentence **they're** would not fit because it means *they are*.

You know (*they're, their*) not happy.   _they're_____

Note that in this case **they're** (they are) fits in with the rest of the sentence.

1. Do they have (*they're, their*) uniforms?   _____

2. By now (*they're, their*) quite tired.   _____

3. Are these (*you're, your*) notes?   _____

4. (*It's, Its*) too late.   _____

5. Is the coat (*her's, hers*)?   _____

6. This is my book. Where is (*yours, your's*)?   _____

7. The cat hurt (*its, it's*) tail.   _____

8. Shall we go in your car or (*our's, ours*)?   _____

9. (*Your, You're*) always complaining.   _____

10. (*Lets, Let's*) go!   _____

lesson 21 Review of Nouns and Pronouns

Read the following:

¹Miles Standish wanted to marry Priscilla Mullins, but he did not have the courage to ask her. ²Instead, Miles sent his friend John Alden to speak for him. ³Miles did not know of John's secret love for Priscilla; in fact, she herself knew nothing of it.

⁴When John brought her the proposal, Priscilla turned it down. ⁵However, she gave him an important hint. ⁶She said: "Why don't you speak for yourself, John?" ⁷Because of his friendship with Miles, he remained silent.

⁸John Alden and Priscilla Mullins were refugees from England who came to America in 1620 on the good ship *Mayflower*. ⁹If you want more information about them, see *The Courtship of Miles Standish* by Henry Wadsworth Longfellow.

EXERCISE 1. Write the antecedents of the following pronouns:

Sample:

he	(sentence 1)	*Miles Standish*
1. *him*	(sentence 2)	
2. *she*	(sentence 3)	
3. *it*	(sentence 3)	
4. *her*	(sentence 4)	
5. *it*	(sentence 4)	
6. *him*	(sentence 5)	
7. *She*	(sentence 6)	
8. *you*	(sentence 6)	
9. *he*	(sentence 7)	
10. *them*	(sentence 9)	

Write:

11. the subject of the verb *brought* in sentence 4: _____

12. the direct object of the verb *brought* in sentence 4: _____

13. the indirect object of the verb *brought* in sentence 4: _____

14. the indirect object of the verb *gave* in sentence 5: _____

15. the direct object of the verb *gave* in sentence 5: _____

In the last paragraph (sentences 8 and 9), there are three common nouns and seven proper nouns. List them in the spaces below.

COMMON NOUNS

16. _____

17. _____

18. _____

PROPER NOUNS

19. _____

20. _____

21. _____

22. _____

23. _____

24. _____

_____

25. _____

_____

EXERCISE 2. Which contraction *beginning with a pronoun* can replace the italicized words? Write your answer in the space provided.

Samples:

You are wasting time.   *You're* _____

Ask her where *the teams are* playing.   *they're* _____

1. *We would* be glad to go along.   _____

2. *It will* take just a minute.   _____

3. Next time *I will* be more careful.   _____

4. Do you know if *he is* home?   _____

5. *It is* none of my business.   _____

6. *My friends and I will* help you.   _____

7. See if *they have* returned.   _____

8. *You have* no time to lose.   _____

9. *Theresa will* be there.   _____

10. *The neighbors are* on vacation.   _____

lesson 22 Action Verbs and Linking Verbs

I. ACTION VERBS

What Is an Action Verb?

An *action verb* **is a verb that expresses action.** There are two kinds of action verbs:

1. Verbs that express *physical action*—action that can be seen or heard:

   The car **skidded, left** the road, and **smashed** into a telephone pole.

   (*Skidded*, *left*, and *smashed* express physical action.)

2. Verbs that express *mental action*—action that takes place in the mind and, therefore, can not be seen or heard:

   We **believed** and **trusted** them because we **knew** them.

   (*Believed*, *trusted*, and *knew* express mental action.)

   Summary: **An** *action verb* **expresses action. The action may be physical or mental.**

EXERCISE 1. If the italicized verb expresses physical action, write **P** in the space provided. If it expresses mental action, write **M**.

Samples:

Pat *tagged* the runner.   P

Did you *understand* the lesson?   M

1. Horace *jogs* before breakfast.   _____

2. I *forgot* the combination.   _____

3. *Do* you *remember* me?   _____

4. Julie *twisted* her ankle. _____

5. *Open* a window. _____

6. Who *rang* the bell? _____

7. The bus *stops* at the corner. _____

8. He *considers* me his best friend. _____

9. We *are hoping* for the best. _____

10. I *dread* the outcome. _____

II. LINKING VERBS

However, not all verbs are action verbs. The verb *is* in the following sentence does not express action. It is a *linking verb*.

Elton *is* angry at us.
L.V.

What Is a Linking Verb?

Note that the verb *is*, in the sentence above, has little meaning of its own. Its main function is to *link* (connect) *Elton* with *angry*. For this reason, we call *is* a *linking verb*.

**A *linking verb* links (connects) the subject with a word
in the predicate that describes or identifies the subject.**

The road *was* slippery.
L.V.

(*Slippery* describes the subject *road*.)

Dolores *is* the captain of the volleyball team.
L.V.

(*Captain* identifies the subject *Dolores*.)

What Are Some Common Linking Verbs?

1. The most frequently used linking verb is *be*, whose forms include the following:

am, are, is, was, were.

Of course, verb phrases ending in *be*, *being*, and *been* are also linking verbs:

will be, would be, are being, have been, could have been, etc.

---

2. In addition, each of the following verbs can be either an action verb or a linking verb, depending on the way it is used.

VERB	USED AS ACTION VERB	USED AS LINKING VERB
appear	The manager *appeared* at 10 a.m.	Fred *appeared* tired.
become	The dress *becomes* (suits) her.	My room *becomes* untidy.
feel	Did you *feel* the cloth?	I *feel* energetic.
grow	Farmers *grow* crops.	The days *grow* longer.
look	We *looked* the place over.	He *looked* unhappy.
smell	I *smelled* smoke.	The air *smelled* salty.
sound	Who *sounded* the alarm?	Her voice *sounded* hoarse.
taste	I *tasted* the soup.	The soup *tasted* delicious.
turn	She *turned* the page.	The weather *turned* cold.

How Can a Linking Verb Be Recognized?

An easy way to tell whether or not a verb is a linking verb is this: if it can be replaced with some form of the verb *be*, it is a linking verb.

Question 1: Is *feels* a linking verb in the following sentence?

Elton *feels* angry.

Answer: We can replace *feels* with *is* (a form of the verb *be*).

Elton *is* angry.

Therefore, *feels*, in the above sentence, is a linking verb.

Question 2: Is *feels* a linking verb in the following sentence?

The patient *feels* pain.

Answer: In this sentence, we cannot replace *feels* with *is*.

Therefore, *feels* here is not a linking verb. It is an action verb.

FURTHER EXAMPLES:

We can replace the verbs below with some form of *be;* this proves they are linking verbs.

1.*a.* Fred **appeared** tired.
(We can say: Fred *was* tired. Therefore, *appeared* is a linking verb.)

2.*a.* The days **grow** longer.
(We can say: The days *are* longer. Therefore, *grow* is a linking verb.)

We cannot replace the verbs below with some form of *be;* this proves they are not linking verbs but action verbs.

1.*b.* The manager **appeared** at 10 a.m.
(We cannot say: The manager *was* at 10 a.m. Therefore, *appeared* in this sentence is an action verb.)

2.*b.* Farmers **grow** crops.
(We cannot say: Farmers *are* crops. Therefore, *grow* in this sentence is an action verb.)

> *Summary:* A *linking verb* connects the subject with a word in the predicate that describes or identifies the subject.

EXERCISE 2. Is the verb in the sentence an action verb or a linking verb? Write your answer in the space provided.

Samples:

Nancy *broke* her arm.   *action*

Joe *looks* tired.   *linking*

1. Today, I *feel* better. _____

2. My grandfather *grew* vegetables. _____

3. This blouse *looks* attractive. _____

4. I *smelled* the fish. _____

5. They *became* lazy. _____

6. Angie *lost* her purse. _____

7. The audience *grew* restless. _____

8. George *tasted* the melon. _____

9. Your cousin *appears* bored. _____

10. Her cookies *tasted* delicious. _____

11. Bruce *dropped* the tools. _____

12. Your voice *sounded* hoarse. _____

13. She *looked* through the whole book. _____

14. I *turned* the dial to the right. _____

15. We *were* exhausted. _____

lesson 23 Helping Verbs and Verb Phrases

What Is a Helping Verb?

Sometimes, as in the following sentence, a verb consists of more than one word.

The letters <u>*have been mailed*</u>.
verb

In *have been mailed*, *mailed* is the **main verb;** *have* and *been* are **helping verbs**.

The letters <u>*have been mailed*</u>.

H.V.   H.V.   M.V.

Helping verbs are verbs that come before and "help" the main verb.

A main verb may have as many as three helping verbs.

ONE HELPING VERB: Anne <u>***has***</u> mailed the letters.
H.V. M.V.

TWO HELPING VERBS: The letters <u>***have been***</u> mailed.
H.V.   H.V.   M.V.

THREE HELPING VERBS: They <u>***should have been***</u> mailed earlier.
H.V.   H.V.   H.V.   M.V.

What Is a Verb Phrase?

When a verb consists of one or more helping verbs plus a main verb, it is called a *verb phrase*.

HELPING VERB(S)   + MAIN VERB = VERB PHRASE

has	+ mailed	= has mailed
have been	+ mailed	= have been mailed
should have been	+ mailed	= should have been mailed

GRAMMAR

Which Verbs Can Be Used as Helping Verbs?

Below is a list of verbs commonly used as helping verbs. Note that *be*, which we studied earlier as a linking verb (page 82), can also be used as a helping verb.

SOME COMMON HELPING VERBS

be, am, are, is,   can, could
   was, were, being, been   will, would
have, has, had   shall, should
do, does, did   must
may, might

EXERCISE 1. Indicate the *verb phrase, helping verb or verbs,* and *main verb* in each of the following sentences.

Sample:

Leaves have been falling all week.

V. PHR. _have been falling_
H.V. _have been_
M.V. _falling_

1. The fire is being investigated.

V. PHR. _____
H.V. _____
M.V. _____

2. The Eagles could have protested the decision.

V. PHR. _____
H.V. _____
M.V. _____

3. You should have seen the mess!

V. PHR. _____
H.V. _____
M.V. _____

4. The patient has improved.

V. PHR. _____
H.V. _____
M.V. _____

5. I must have left my wallet at home.

V. PHR. _____
H.V. _____
M.V. _____

6. Harvey has been acting strangely lately.

V. PHR. _____
H.V. _____
M.V. _____

7. They have played basketball for two seasons.

    V. PHR. _____

    H.V. _____

    M.V. _____

8. At last the constitution has been approved.

    V. PHR. _____

    H.V. _____

    M.V. _____

9. We might have scored in the first inning.

    V. PHR. _____

    H.V. _____

    M.V. _____

10. All of the tickets may have been sold by now.

    V. PHR. _____

    H.V. _____

    M.V. _____

Word Order in Questions

In questions, we usually put the subject after the first helping verb.

> **Are tickets** being collected?
> H.V.   S.

(The subject *tickets* comes after the first helping verb *Are*.)

> **Has Joanne** given her talk?
> H.V.   S.

(The subject *Joanne* comes after the helping verb *Has*.)

EXERCISE 2. Change the following statements to questions.

Sample:

The tire has been repaired.   *Has the tire been repaired?*

1. The argument has been settled. _____

2. Ernie will buy the refreshments. _____

3. It has been raining all day. _____

4. We should have waited a bit longer. _____

5. Our team could have done better. _____

Reminder: **Did you end each of your questions above with a question mark?**

Composition Hint

Shorten your verb phrases whenever possible. Avoid *wordiness*—the use of unnecessary words. Aim for *conciseness*—brief, uncluttered expression.

WORDY: If you do not run for president, she ***may run***.

CONCISE: If you do not run for president, she ***may***.

         (The main verb *run* is understood.)

WORDY: Jim refused to apologize. He ***should have apologized***.

CONCISE: Jim refused to apologize. He ***should have***.

         (The main verb *apologized* is understood.)

WORDY: They are not being blamed, but I ***am being blamed***.

CONCISE: They are not being blamed, but I ***am***.

         (The helping verb *being* and the main verb *blamed* are understood.)

EXERCISE 3.   Make each of the following sentences more concise by shortening a verb phrase.

Sample:

I could have waited, and perhaps I should have waited.

I could have waited, and perhaps I should have.

1. She does not have to go, but I must go.

2. They were supposed to be paid; they were not paid.

3. If Sharon does not complain, no one else will complain.

4. My word is being questioned, but your word is not being questioned.

5. We did not quit, though we should have quit.

EXERCISE 4. In each sentence below, one or more italicized helping verbs are used in place of a full verb phrase. Write the full verb phrase in the space provided.

Sample:

The forecaster said it would not rain, but it *did*.   <u>*did rain*</u>

1. Fred did not come, though he *could have*.   _____

2. You are not being accused. I *am*.   _____

3. Gina doubts she can win, but I think she *can*.   _____

4. No one can tell me what I should not do and what I *should*.   _____

5. If you hadn't answered, I *would have*.   _____

Question: Is the verb in the following sentence *mailed* or *have been mailed?*

The letters have been mailed.

Answer: *have been mailed.*

Important: Whenever you are asked for the verb of a sentence containing a verb phrase, *give the whole verb phrase.*

EXERCISE 5. Name the verb in each of the following sentences.

Sample:

They must have lost their way.   <u>*must have lost*</u>

1. Anything can happen.   _____

2. You might have tried harder.   _____

3. Is the rubbish being removed?   _____

4. They should have been invited.   _____

5. Jack should have been given another chance.   _____

lesson 24 Verbs in Contractions

A friend with whom you are to have lunch asks whether you would rather eat at twelve or at one. To you, it does not matter.

Which of the following answers would you probably give your friend?

1. It does not matter.
2. It doesn't matter.

You would probably say: **It doesn't matter.**

In informal conversation, we tend to combine *does* with *not*, forming the contraction *doesn't*. **A *contraction*, as we learned on page 76, is a combination of two words, with one or more letters omitted.**

Note that *not*, the second word in the contraction, loses the letter *o*, and in place of that *o* we have an apostrophe: **doesn't.**

In contractions consisting of a verb plus *not*, *not* loses an *o*.

VERB	+ NOT	= CONTRACTION	LETTERS OMITTED
is	+ not	= *isn't*	*o*
are	+ not	= *aren't*	*o*
would	+ not	= *wouldn't*	*o*

In one case, *not* loses an *n* and an *o:*

can	+ not	= *can't*	*n o*

Finally, learn this irregular (unusual) contraction:

will	+ not	= *won't*

EXERCISE 1. Write the contraction.

Sample:

have   + not = ___*haven't*___

1. has   + not = _____   6. is   + not = _____
2. are   + not = _____   7. do   + not = _____
3. must   + not = _____   8. will + not = _____
4. can   + not = _____   9. did   + not = _____
5. should + not = _____   10. does + not = _____

EXERCISE 2. What letter or letters have been omitted in forming the following contractions?

Samples:

couldn't _____ *o* _____

I'll _____ *wi* _____

1. wouldn't _____
2. we've _____
3. can't _____
4. they're _____
5. hadn't _____

6. you'd _____
7. didn't _____
8. I've _____
9. let's _____
10. it's _____

Contractions are entirely natural and correct in *informal* English (friendly notes, everyday conversation). However, they are not ordinarily used in *formal* English (business letters, letters of application, reports).

EXERCISE 3. Change each of the following contractions to *formal* English.

Samples:

didn't _____ *did not* _____

I've _____ *I have* _____

1. hasn't _____
2. isn't _____
3. won't _____
4. I'll _____
5. shouldn't _____

6. can't _____
7. weren't _____
8. you'd _____
9. wasn't _____
10. it's _____

The contraction *ain't* is considered nonstandard. This means that *ain't* should not be used in either formal or informal English situations. Avoid *ain't*.

INSTEAD OF	USE
I *ain't* ready.	**I'm not ready.** or **I am not ready.**
Ain't I next?	**Am I not next?**
They *ain't* come back.	**They haven't come back.** or **They have not come back.**
Ain't you afraid?	**Aren't you afraid?** or **Are you not afraid?**

EXERCISE 4. What would you use instead of the italicized word or words in each sentence below? Give two answers—one for an informal English situation, and one for a formal English situation.

Samples:

NONSTANDARD:	You *ain't* in charge.
INFORMAL:	You *aren't* in charge.
FORMAL:	You *are not* in charge.

NONSTANDARD:	*Ain't it* a pity?
INFORMAL:	*Isn't it* a pity?
FORMAL:	*Is it not* a pity?

NONSTANDARD:	I *ain't* hungry.
INFORMAL:	*I'm not* hungry.
FORMAL:	I *am not* hungry.

NONSTANDARD:	He *ain't* been well.
INFORMAL:	He *hasn't* been well.
FORMAL:	He *has not* been well.

1. NONSTANDARD: She *ain't* home.

   INFORMAL: _____

   FORMAL: _____

2. NONSTANDARD: They *ain't* going.

   INFORMAL: _____

   FORMAL: _____

3. NONSTANDARD: I *ain't* through yet.

   INFORMAL: _____

   FORMAL: _____

4. NONSTANDARD: *Ain't you* sold that car?

   INFORMAL: _____

   FORMAL: _____

5. NONSTANDARD: She *ain't* said a word.

   INFORMAL: _____

   FORMAL: _____

6. NONSTANDARD: *Ain't it* a shame?

   INFORMAL: _____

   FORMAL: _____

7. NONSTANDARD: *Ain't he* been paid?

INFORMAL: _____

FORMAL: _____

8. NONSTANDARD: *Ain't she* your friend?

INFORMAL: _____

FORMAL: _____

9. NONSTANDARD: We *ain't* been to town.

INFORMAL: _____

FORMAL: _____

10. NONSTANDARD: You *ain't* heard anything yet.

INFORMAL: _____

FORMAL: _____

lesson 25 Adjectives

Question 1: What is the difference between *sweater* and *that white turtleneck sweater?*

Answer: *Sweater* means any sweater at all.

That, white, and *turtleneck* **modify** (change) the meaning of *sweater* from any sweater to one particular sweater.

That, white, and *turtleneck* are **modifiers** because they change (modify) the meaning of *sweater.*

More exactly, *that, white,* and *turtleneck* are **adjectives** because the word they modify —*sweater*—is a noun.

Question 2: What is an *adjective?*

Answer: **An *adjective* is a word that modifies a noun or a pronoun.**

1. *Light* rain fell.
   ADJ. N.

   The adjective *Light* modifies the noun *rain.*

2. Joan wore *red* shoes.
   ADJ. N.

   The adjective *red* modifies the noun *shoes.*

3. He was *angry.*
   PRON.   ADJ.

   The adjective *angry* modifies the pronoun *He.*

Adjectives give information by answering such questions as *What kind? Which one? How many? Whose?*

WHAT KIND?	*blue* sky, *rainy* day, *early* riser
WHICH ONE?	*this* book, *first* job, *second* floor
HOW MANY?	*four* girls, *many* reasons, *few* failures
WHOSE?	*my* brother, *your* face, *his* wallet

Question 3: How many adjectives are there in the following?

Two husky, rough-coated dogs trotted out as we approached the farmhouse, and we called to them in a friendly way, but they were watchful and suspicious.

Answer: Eight.

(1) *Two,*
(2) *husky,* and
(3) *rough-coated*   modify the noun *dogs;*

(4) *the*   modifies the noun *farmhouse;*

(5) *a* and
(6) *friendly*   modify the noun *way;*

(7) *watchful* and
(8) *suspicious*   modify the pronoun *they.*

Note: *The, a,* and *an,* the most frequently encountered of all adjectives, are called **articles.** Since they appear so often, let us agree to exclude them when identifying adjectives.

EXERCISE 1. In each sentence below, find an adjective and explain what it modifies.

Samples:

We sat in the first row.

ADJ. _*first*_____ modifies _N. *row*_____.

She was unhappy.

ADJ. _*unhappy*_____ modifies _PRON. *She*_____.

1. Turn to the last page.

ADJ. _____ modifies _____.

2. They were early.

ADJ. _____ modifies _____.

3. Does Alma have blue eyes?

ADJ. _____ modifies _____.

4. Ted had no money.

ADJ. _____ modifies _____.

5. Two birds flew into the trees.

ADJ. _____ modifies _____.

6. The roads are slippery.

   ADJ. _____ modifies _____.

7. Are the rolls fresh?

   ADJ. _____ modifies _____.

8. You look pale.

   ADJ. _____ modifies _____.

9. Saturday was a busy day.

   ADJ. _____ modifies _____.

10. We had a beautiful sunset.

    ADJ. _____ modifies _____.

11. The noise was ear-splitting.

    ADJ. _____ modifies _____.

12. I am hungry.

    ADJ. _____ modifies _____.

13. Warmer weather is on the way.

    ADJ. _____ modifies _____.

14. Do you have a gray cat?

    ADJ. _____ modifies _____.

15. The results were poor.

    ADJ. _____ modifies _____.

16. It was a delicious meal.

    ADJ. _____ modifies _____.

17. A curly-haired boy entered.

    ADJ. _____ modifies _____.

18. We were fortunate.

    ADJ. _____ modifies _____.

19. Sue has three brothers.

    ADJ. _____ modifies _____.

20. Thirty people applied for the job.

    ADJ. _____ modifies _____.

Proper Adjectives

You will recall that proper nouns (*Canada, Shakespeare*, etc.) are capitalized. (See page 38.) The adjectives formed from proper nouns (*Canadian, Shakespearean*, etc.) are capitalized, too. They are called **proper adjectives.** Here are some proper nouns and the proper adjectives that can be formed from them.

PROPER NOUN	PROPER ADJECTIVE
China	*Chinese* food
Jefferson	*Jeffersonian* democracy
Egypt	*Egyptian* pyramids
France	*French* perfume
Rome	*Roman* arch

Composition Hint

Make your writing more concise by replacing a wordy expression with an adjective.

WORDY: The diplomat visited several nations *on the continent of Africa.*

CONCISE: The diplomat visited several **African** nations.
ADJ.

WORDY: Avoid decisions *that are made in haste.*

CONCISE: Avoid **hasty** decisions.
ADJ.

EXERCISE 2. Rewrite the sentence, using an adjective instead of the italicized expression.

Sample:

Many dealers sell products *manufactured in Japan.*

Many dealers sell Japanese products.

1. *Olives imported from Spain* are sold in supermarkets.

_____

2. They spoke in words *that were full of bitterness.*

_____

3. I read an article about Eskimos *who live in Canada.*

_____

4. She gave me a look *that showed anger*.

_____

5. Coffee *grown in Brazil* is quite expensive.

_____

6. He never makes a move *that involves risk*.

_____

7. Most cars *built in America* are heavier than foreign cars.

_____

8. In every town there are people *who suffer from loneliness*.

_____

9. You are lucky to have neighbors *who show kindness*.

_____

10. What is the name of the ambassador *from the Commonwealth of Australia?*

_____

Another Composition Hint

Before using an adjective, make sure that it is needed.

QUESTION: What is wrong with the following sentence?

We want the true facts.

ANSWER: The adjective *true* is not needed because all facts are true. The sentence should read:

We want the facts.

EXERCISE 3. Which adjectives should be removed because they are unnecessary?

Sample:

Put some cold ice cubes into the lemonade.   *cold*

1. I was a stupid fool.   _____

2. A young, rich millionaire has bought the painting.   _____

3. We were never told the real truth.   _____

4. Antony wept at the sight of Caesar's dead corpse.   _____

5. Draw a round circle. _____

6. White snow began falling. _____

7. There is a plentiful abundant supply of potatoes. _____

8. The end result was that we lost the game. _____

9. Do you own any old antiques? _____

10. Many modern women of today have their own careers. _____

11. One person slept throughout the entire performance. _____

12. They visit hospitals to cheer up sick invalids. _____

13. It happened on a summer evening in July. _____

14. A cold icy wind is blowing from the northeast. _____

15. Mona inherited some money from a rich well-to-do uncle. _____

lesson 26 Predicate Adjectives and Predicate Nouns

In some sentences, all we need to make a complete statement is a subject and a verb.

> Birds fly.
> S.   V.

> John smiled.
> S.   V.

But in other sentences, a subject and a verb may not be enough, especially if the verb is a linking verb.

> 1. The milk *tastes* . . .
> S.   L.V.

> 2. Andy *is* . . .
> S. L.V.

In each of the above two sentences, we must add a **complement—a "completing" word or expression**—to the linking verb. For example:

> 1. The milk tastes *sour.*
> L.V.

> (The adjective *sour* is a *complement* of the linking verb *tastes.*)

> 2. Andy is the *owner.*
> L.V.

> (The noun *owner* is a *complement* of the linking verb *is.*)

EXERCISE 1. Add a suitable complement to each linking verb below to complete the sentence. You may choose your complements from the following list:

juicy	easy	louder	fishy
tall	delicious	criminals	water
money	painters	gray	vehciles
islands			

Sample:

Oranges *are* __juicy_____.
     L.V.

1. Oaks *grow* _____.
     L.V.

2. Thieves *are* _____.
     L.V.

3. The cake *looked* _____.
     L.V.

4. Ice *becomes* _____.
     L.V.

5. The beach *smelled* _____.
     L.V.

6. Time *is* _____.
     L.V.

7. His hair *turned* _____.
     L.V.

8. Cars and trucks *are* _____.
     L.V.

9. Rembrandt and Picasso *were* _____.
     L.V.

10. The test *seems* _____.
     L.V.

11. The noise *became* _____.
     L.V.

12. Iceland and Greenland *are* _____.
     L.V.

In the exercise you have just done, you used twelve complements to complete twelve linking verbs. You probably realize that you have been using complements all your life without knowing that they were complements.

There are several kinds of complements. In this lesson we shall study two of them:

     1. the *predicate adjective*, and

     2. the *predicate noun*.

I. PREDICATE ADJECTIVES

Question: What is a *predicate adjective?*

Answer: **A *predicate adjective* is an adjective that completes a linking verb and modifies the subject of that linking verb.**

Examples: 1. The soup *tastes* **salty.**
                S.   L.V.   PRED. ADJ.

(*Salty* is a predicate adjective because it completes the linking verb *tastes* and modifies the subject *soup.*)

2. You *were* **marvelous.**
    S.   L.V.   PRED. ADJ.

(*Marvelous* is a predicate adjective because it completes the linking verb *were* and modifies the subject *You.*)

EXERCISE 2.   In each sentence below, find the *linking verb,* the *predicate adjective,* and the word that the predicate adjective *modifies.*

Samples:

The children grew restless.   L.V. _____ *grew* _____
                               PRED. ADJ. _____ *restless* _____
                               MODIFIES _____ *children* _____

She has been helpful.   L.V. _____ *has been* _____
                               PRED. ADJ. _____ *helpful* _____
                               MODIFIES _____ *She* _____

1. We are ready.   L.V. _____
                               PRED. ADJ. _____
                               MODIFIES _____

2. The cellar smells damp.   L.V. _____
                               PRED. ADJ. _____
                               MODIFIES _____

3. Their story sounded strange. L.V. _____
                               PRED. ADJ. _____
                               MODIFIES _____

4. Did they seem unhappy? L.V. _____

PRED. ADJ. _____

MODIFIES _____

5. Laura looked annoyed. L.V. _____

PRED. ADJ. _____

MODIFIES _____

6. Her friend has been ill. L.V. _____

PRED. ADJ. _____

MODIFIES _____

7. My hands were wet. L.V. _____

PRED. ADJ. _____

MODIFIES _____

8. Your appetite seems good. L.V. _____

PRED. ADJ. _____

MODIFIES _____

9. He must have been angry. L.V. _____

PRED. ADJ. _____

MODIFIES _____

10. These vegetables taste fresh. L.V. _____

PRED. ADJ. _____

MODIFIES _____

II. PREDICATE NOUNS

Question: What is a *predicate noun*?

Answer: **A *predicate noun* is a noun that completes a linking verb and explains the subject of that linking verb.**

Rose *is* my ***cousin***.
S. L.V.   PRED. N.

(*Cousin* is a predicate noun because it completes
the linking verb *is* and explains the subject *Rose*.)

Here are some further examples of predicate nouns.

A kitten *becomes* a **cat**.
S.   L.V.   PRED. N.

Fred *will be* our **driver**.
S.   L.V.   PRED. N.

The expedition *was* a **failure**.
S.   L.V.   PRED. N.

EXERCISE 3. In each sentence below, find the *subject*, the *linking verb*, and the *predicate noun* that explains the subject.

Sample:

Australia is a continent.

SUBJ.	*Australia*
L.V.	*is*
PRED. N.	*continent*

1. Copper is a metal.

SUBJ. _____
L.V. _____
PRED. N. _____

2. The water became steam.

SUBJ. _____
L.V. _____
PRED. N. _____

3. Was Marie the umpire?

SUBJ. _____
L.V. _____
PRED. N. _____

4. You may become an inventor.

SUBJ. _____
L.V. _____
PRED. N. _____

5. Mars is a planet.

SUBJ. _____
L.V. _____
PRED. N. _____

6. This desert was once a valley.   SUBJ. _____

                                                      L.V. _____

                                                      PRED. N. _____

7. Julio has been captain for a year.   SUBJ. _____

    L.V. _____

    PRED. N. _____

8. Is the cat a nuisance?   SUBJ. _____

    L.V. _____

    PRED. N. _____

9. The flood could have been a disaster.   SUBJ. _____

    L.V. _____

    PRED. N. _____

10. The pie will be our dessert.   SUBJ. _____

    L.V. _____

    PRED. N. _____

Composition Hint

> We often have a choice when we explain or describe a subject: we can use either (1) a predicate noun, or (2) a predicate adjective.
>
> 1. I was a *fool*.
>   PRED. N.
>
>   (The predicate noun *fool* describes the subject *I*.)
>
> 2. I was *foolish*.
>   PRED. ADJ.
>
>   (The predicate adjective *foolish* describes the subject *I*.)
>
> Become familiar with both of the above choices. As a result, when you write, you will be able to select the one that better expresses your idea in a particular situation.

EXERCISE 4. Rewrite each sentence, changing the predicate noun to a predicate adjective.

Sample:

Joan is a wonder.
  Joan is wonderful.
_____

1. The play was a success.
_____

2. Pete has never been a friend.
_____

3. My desk is a mess.
_____

4. The news was a surprise.
_____

5. Was the outcome a shock?
_____

EXERCISE 5. Rewrite each sentence, changing the predicate adjective to a predicate noun.

Sample:

Ben was sensational.
  Ben was a sensation.
_____

1. You were cowardly.
_____

2. Gambling can be risky.
_____

3. He was brutal.
_____

4. The pup is beautiful.
_____

5. Don't be bossy.
_____

lesson 27 Review: Nouns, Verbs, and Adjectives

To learn what part of speech a word is, ask yourself: How is the word used in its sentence?

Here, for example, is what you would have to do to learn what part of speech *paper* is in three different sentences:

1. I need more **_paper._**
   N.

   (*Paper* names a thing and is the direct object of the verb *need; paper* is a **noun.**)

2. The room will look better if we **_paper_** the walls.
   V.

   (*Paper* expresses action; *paper* is a **verb.**)

3. Have you any **_paper_** clips?
   ADJ.

   (*Paper* modifies the noun *clips*—it tells what kind of *clips; paper* is an **adjective.**)

EXERCISE 1. What part of speech is the italicized word?

Samples:

The child played with her *toy* piano.	*adjective*
An instrument panel is not a *toy*.	*noun*
You may damage the hi-fi if you *toy* with the controls.	*verb*

1. We live in *California*. _____
2. *California* oranges are cheaper today. _____

3. Raise your right *hand*. _____
4. This *hand* lotion prevents chapping. _____
5. Please *hand* me the hammer. _____

6. *Leather* is a natural material. _____
7. These shoes have *leather* soles. _____

8. She *injured* her ankle. _____

9. Is your *injured* elbow better? _____

10. The *injured* were rushed to the hospital. _____

11. Have you tasted *Florida* corn? _____

12. *Florida* was once a Spanish territory. _____

13. Who is the *head* counselor? _____

14. Hold your *head* high. _____

15. *Head* east for two miles. _____

16. His pockets were *empty*. _____

17. Please *empty* the wastebasket. _____

18. *Telephone* me in the morning. _____

19. Did the *telephone* ring? _____

20. The *telephone* bill has not been paid. _____

21. *Clear* the field. _____

22. It was a *clear* day. _____

23. The *light* went out. _____

24. Shall we *light* the candles now? _____

25. I had a *light* breakfast. _____

Read the following passage:

Kino, a young Mexican diver, finds a beautiful rare pearl. It is very large. Immediately, word spreads in the village that he will be rich. But when Kino tries to sell the pearl, the dishonest buyers tell him it is worthless. They offer him a ridiculous price. Kino refuses to sell.

Then, murderous thieves fall upon Kino, in broad daylight as well as at night. They fail to get the pearl. Kino kills one attacker. Others, however, burn Kino's poor hut to the ground.

Kino decides to go to Mexico City, the distant capital, to try to sell the pearl. On a dark and windy night, with brave wife Juana and infant son Coyotito, he sets out on the long, dangerous journey.

They have not walked many miles, when, in the dim distance, Kino detects three approaching figures: a man on horseback and two trackers on foot. Across the saddle, a long metal object gleams in the sun. It is a rifle.

For the full story of Kino, Juana, and Coyotito, read *The Pearl*, a fascinating short novel by John Steinbeck.

EXERCISE 2. There are thirty adjectives in the passage you have just read, not counting *a*, *an*, and *the*. List these adjectives in the order in which they occur, and indicate the words they modify. The first five answers have been filled in as samples.

	ADJECTIVE	WORD MODIFIED
1.	young	diver
2.	Mexican	diver
3.	beautiful	pearl
4.	rare	pearl
5.	large	It
6.		
7.		
8.		
9.		
10.		
11.		
12.		
13.		
14.		
15.		
16.		
17.		
18.		
19.		
20.		
21.		
22.		
23.		
24.		
25.		
26.		
27.		
28.		
29.		
30.		

lesson 28 Adverbs

If some reporter were to describe the weather for us by stating merely,

"It snowed,"

we would not be entirely satisfied.

Certain questions would arise. For example, we would want to know:

1. *How*, or *to what extent*, did it snow?   Our reporter could have said:

"It snowed *heavily*," or
"It snowed *moderately*," or
"It snowed *lightly*."

2. *When* did it snow?   Our reporter could have said:

"It snowed *yesterday*," or
"It snowed *today*," or
"It snowed *Thursday*."

3. *Where* did it snow?   Our reporter could have said:

"It snowed *locally*," or
"It snowed *upstate*," or
"It snowed *inland*."

All of the italicized words above, the words that tell *how*, *when*, or *where*, are adverbs.

If our reporter had used some adverbs—for example, if he or she had said,

"It snowed *heavily yesterday upstate*,"

we would have had a better idea of the weather.

What Is an Adverb?

An *adverb* is a word that modifies either

a verb, or
an adjective, or
another adverb.

Let us take up these uses of an adverb one at a time.

I. An adverb is a word that modifies a verb.

The Pirates *played **brilliantly**.*
         V.   ADV.

(*Brilliantly* is an adverb because it modifies the verb *played*.)

The Giants *fielded **skillfully**.*
         V.   ADV.

(*Skillfully* is an adverb because it modifies the verb *fielded*.)

Both teams *performed **well**.*
         V.   ADV.

(*Well* is an adverb because it modifies the verb *performed*.)

The Dodgers *did **not** play.*
         V. ADV. V.

(*Not* is an adverb because it modifies the verb *did play*.)

They *are playing **tomorrow**.*
      V.   ADV.

(*Tomorrow* is an adverb because it modifies the verb *are playing*.)

They *will play **here**.*
       V.   ADV.

(*Here* is an adverb because it modifies the verb *will play*.)

Most adverbs answer one of the following questions: HOW? WHEN? WHERE? TO WHAT EXTENT?

The Pirates played ***brilliantly***.
            ADV.

(*Brilliantly* tells HOW the Pirates played.)

They are playing ***tomorrow***.
          ADV.

(*Tomorrow* tells WHEN they are playing.)

They will play ***here***.
       ADV.

(*Here* tells WHERE they will play.)

They have ***fully*** recovered from
      ADV.
their slump.

(*Fully* tells TO WHAT EXTENT they have recovered.)

EXERCISE 1. Find the adverb and the verb that it modifies.

Samples:

Your money will be refunded immediately.

The ADV. _____immediately_____ modifies the V. _____will be refunded_____.

Yesterday I broke my glasses.

The ADV. _____Yesterday_____ modifies the V. _____broke_____.

1. The damage was repaired quickly.

The ADV. _____ modifies the V. _____.

2. Bill usually brings his lunch.   The ADV. _____ modifies

the V. _____.

3. The clock stopped suddenly.   The ADV. _____ modifies

the V. _____.

4. We are leaving soon.   The ADV. _____ modifies

the V. _____.

5. The engine sometimes backfires.   The ADV. _____ modifies

the V. _____.

6. Look in the closet. Is your coat there?   The ADV. _____ modifies

the V. _____.

7. The carpenters have not completed their work.   The ADV. _____ modifies

the V. _____.

8. Remove the cover carefully.   The ADV. _____ modifies

the V. _____.

9. Did the visitors stay long?   The ADV. _____ modifies

the V. _____.

10. Rarely does Nancy make a mistake.   The ADV. _____ modifies

the V. _____.

II. An adverb is a word that modifies an adjective.

A _very_ odd thing happened.
ADV. ADJ.

(_Very_ is an adverb because it modifies the adjective _odd_.)

The cobra is a **_highly_** poisonous snake.
ADV.   ADJ.

(_Highly_ is an adverb because it modifies the adjective _poisonous_.)

A window was **_partly_** open.
ADV.   ADJ.

(_Partly_ is an adverb because it modifies the predicate adjective _open_.)

EXERCISE 2. Find the adverb and the adjective that it modifies.

Sample:

You were absolutely right.   The ADV. _absolutely_ modifies

the ADJ. _right_.

1. They were very lucky.   The ADV. _____ modifies
                                    the ADJ. _____ .

2. An unusually large crowd gath-   The ADV. _____ modifies
   ered.   the ADJ. _____ .

3. Is the soup too hot?   The ADV. _____ modifies
                                    the ADJ. _____ .

4. They had a quite inexpensive   The ADV. _____ modifies
   meal.   the ADJ. _____ .

5. Freshly poured concrete hardens The ADV. _____ modifies
   in a few hours.   the ADJ. _____ .

III. An adverb is a word that modifies another adverb.

The fight began ***quite*** *unexpectedly*.   (*Quite* is an adverb because it modifies the
      ADV.   ADV.   adverb *unexpectedly*.)

I ***very*** *quietly* closed the door.   (*Very* is an adverb because it modifies the
ADV. ADV.   adverb *quietly*.)

Both teams played ***extremely*** *well*.   (*Extremely* is an adverb because it modifies
      ADV.   ADV.   the adverb *well*.)

EXERCISE 3. Find the two adverbs in the sentence, and explain why each is an adverb.

Sample:

Our plants are doing ex-   (*a*) _*Extremely*_ is an adverb because
tremely well.   it modifies the _*adverb well*_ .

                            (*b*) _*Well*_ is an adverb because
                                 it modifies the _*verb are doing*_ .

1. You reported the details   (*a*) _____ is an adverb because
   quite accurately.   it modifies the _____ .

                              (*b*) _____ is an adverb because
                                   it modifies the _____ .

2. Alex very cleverly kept out   (*a*) _____ is an adverb because
   of the argument.   it modifies the _____ .

                                 (*b*) _____ is an adverb because
                                      it modifies the _____ .

3. Lightning flashed and rain fell shortly afterwards.

(a) _____ is an adverb because it modifies the _____.

(b) _____ is an adverb because it modifies the _____.

4. He swings at the ball too soon.

(a) _____ is an adverb because it modifies the _____.

(b) _____ is an adverb because it modifies the _____.

5. I left at noon, but Shirley had left somewhat earlier.

(a) _____ is an adverb because it modifies the _____.

(b) _____ is an adverb because it modifies the _____.

> *Summary:* **An adverb is a word that modifies**
> **a verb, or**
> **an adjective, or**
> **another adverb.**

EXERCISE 4. Explain why the italicized word is an adverb.

Samples:

You acted *wisely*.	_Wisely_ modifies the	_v. acted_ .
You acted *very* wisely.	_Very_ modifies the	_adv. wisely_ .
You were *very* wise.	_Very_ modifies the	_adj. wise_ .

1. She poured the soup *carefully*. _____ modifies the _____.

2. She poured *quite* carefully. _____ modifies the _____.

3. She was *quite* careful. _____ modifies the _____.

4. The apple was *partly* rotten. _____ modifies the _____.

5. They behaved *strangely*. _____ modifies the _____.

6. I was *furiously* angry. _____ modifies the _____.

7. Please walk *more* slowly. _____ modifies the _____.

8. The quarrel has *not* ended. _____ modifies the _____.

9. Were you *really* afraid? _____ modifies the _____.

10. Do not begin *too* suddenly. _____ modifies the _____.

lesson 29 Forming Adverbs From Adjectives

I. Most adverbs are formed by adding *ly* to an adjective.

ADJECTIVE   ADVERB

skillful + ly = skillfully
brave   + ly = bravely

EXERCISE 1.   Change the following adjectives to adverbs.

Sample: dangerous   *dangerously* _____

    1. fearless   _____

    2. clever   _____

    3. foolish   _____

    4. wonderful   _____

In the above exercise, we formed adverbs by adding *ly* directly to an adjective. But in some cases, as in II and III that follow, we must make a change in the adjective before adding *ly*.

II. If an adjective ends in *ic*, add *al* before adding *ly*.

basic   + al + ly = basically
terrific + al + ly = terrifically

EXERCISE 2.   Change the following adjectives to adverbs.

Sample: drastic   *drastically* _____

    1. tragic   _____

    2. democratic   _____

    3. hectic   _____

    4. romantic   _____

III. If an adjective ends in *y*, change the *y* to *i* and then add *ly*.

$$\text{easy} \longrightarrow [\text{easi}] + \text{ly} = \text{easily}$$
$$\text{noisy} \longrightarrow [\text{noisi}] + \text{ly} = \text{noisily}$$

EXERCISE 3.   Change the following adjectives to adverbs.

Sample: happy   _happily_

1. angry   _____
2. greedy   _____
3. lazy   _____
4. hungry   _____
5. hasty   _____

IV. If an adjective ends in *le*, do not add *ly*; simply change *le* to *ly*.

$$\text{able} - \text{ably}$$
$$\text{gentle} - \text{gently}$$

EXERCISE 4.   Change the following adjectives to adverbs.

Sample: simple   _simply_

1. probable   _____
2. noble   _____
3. idle   _____
4. ample   _____
5. capable   _____

Show that you have understood this lesson by doing the following two review exercises.

EXERCISE 5.   Change the following adjectives to adverbs.

ADJECTIVE	ADVERB	ADJECTIVE	ADVERB
1. eager	_____	7. sharp	_____
2. normal	_____	8. busy	_____
3. courageous	_____	9. economic	_____
4. fierce	_____	10. helpless	_____
5. quiet	_____	11. annual	_____
6. final	_____	12. steady	_____

13. real	_____		17. possible	_____
14. favorable	_____		18. unhappy	_____
15. respectful	_____		19. unusual	_____
16. scientific	_____		20. comfortable	_____

EXERCISE 6. Change the following adverbs to adjectives.

	ADVERB	ADJECTIVE
Samples:	definitely	*definite*
	ably	*able*
1.	joyously	_____
2.	gradually	_____
3.	unluckily	_____
4.	naturally	_____
5.	recklessly	_____
6.	unfortunately	_____
7.	strongly	_____
8.	excellently	_____
9.	basically	_____
10.	simply	_____

Composition Hint

Adverbs can often help us express ourselves more concisely. Compare the following:

> WORDY: You worked *in a careless manner*.

> CONCISE: You worked *carelessly*.

EXERCISE 7. Express the following thoughts more concisely. *Hint:* Change the italicized expression to an adverb ending in **ly**.

Samples:

The motor runs *with a noisy sound*.
  The motor runs noisily.

Under normal conditions, we leave at 3 P.M.
  Normally, we leave at 3 P.M.

1. They behaved *in a strange way*.

   _____

2. *Under usual circumstances*, the train is on time.

   _____

3. He acted *like a foolish person*.

   _____

4. *All of a sudden*, the lights went out.

   _____

5. My heart was beating *at a rapid rate*.

   _____

6. *It is probable that* you will soon feel better.

   _____

7. Our meetings are conducted *in a democratic way*.

   _____

8. *In an angry voice*, she demanded that we leave at once.

   _____

9. Try to explain the problem *in simple language*.

   _____

10. *From a financial point of view*, the business is sound.

    _____

lesson 30 Recognizing Adverbs and Adjectives

I.   It is a mistake to think that a word is an adverb just because it ends in **ly**. To tell whether or not a particular word is an adverb, we must check to see how that word is used in its sentence.

Question: Is *weekly* an adverb in this sentence?

1. The workers receive a *weekly* salary.

Answer: No.

Reason: *Weekly* modifies the noun *salary*. A word that modifies a noun is an *adjective*. Therefore, *weekly*, in sentence 1, is an *adjective*.

Question: Is *weekly* an adverb in the following sentence?

2. The workers are paid *weekly*.

Answer: Yes.

Reason: *Weekly* modifies the verb *are paid*. A word that modifies a verb is an *adverb*. Therefore, in sentence 2, *weekly* is an *adverb*.

EXERCISE 1.   Is the italicized word an adverb or an adjective? *Hint:* Before giving your answer, check to see how the italicized word is used in its sentence.

Samples:

Today the mail came *early*.   <u>adverb</u>

We had an *early* dinner.   <u>adjective</u>

1. We pay the rent *monthly*.   _____

2. How much is your *monthly* telephone bill?   _____

3. They had a *lively* discussion.   _____

4. Step *lively*.   _____

GRAMMAR   *119*

5. Do you read a newspaper *daily?* _____

6. Dad left for his *daily* trip to the office. _____

7. We walked *leisurely*. _____

8. I spent a *leisurely* weekend at home. _____

9. What is the minimum *hourly* wage? _____

10. The patient's temperature was checked *hourly*. _____

II.   Some words that do not end in **ly**—for example, *long* and *fast*—can be adverbs or adjectives. Again, we must check to see how such words are used in their sentences before saying that they are adverbs or adjectives.

Question: Is *long* an adverb in this sentence?

3. Did you wait *long?*

Answer: Yes.

Reason: *Long* modifies the verb *did wait*. A word that modifies a verb is an *adverb*. Therefore, in sentence 3, *long* is an *adverb*.

Question: Is *long* an adverb in the following sentence?

4. They are going on a *long* trip.

Answer: No.

Reason: *Long* modifies the noun *trip*. A word that modifies a noun is an *adjective*. Therefore, *long*, in sentence 4, is an *adjective*.

EXERCISE 2.   Indicate whether the italicized word is an adverb or an adjective, and tell what it modifies.

Samples:

The clock is *fast*.   *Fast* is an ___*adjective*___
                        modifying the ___*N.*___ ___*clock*___.

She runs *fast*.   *Fast* is an ___*adverb*___
                        modifying the ___*V.*___ ___*runs*___.

1. These shoes are *tight*.   *Tight* is an _____
                              modifying the _____ _____.

2. You closed the jar *tight*.   *Tight* is an _____
                                 modifying the _____ _____.

3. We made the *right* choice.   *Right* is an _____

      modifying the _____ _____.

4. I turned *right*.   *Right* is an _____

      modifying the _____ _____.

5. The patient is *well*.   *Well* is an _____

      modifying the _____ _____.

6. They sang *well*.   *Well* is an _____

      modifying the _____ _____.

7. A plane flew *low*.   *Low* is an _____

      modifying the _____ _____.

8. The price was *low*.   *Low* is an _____

      modifying the _____ _____.

9. Mary is a *close* friend.   *Close* is an _____

      modifying the _____ _____.

10. My hair was cut *close*.   *Close* is an _____

      modifying the _____ _____.

11. Jack works *hard*.   *Hard* is an _____

      modifying the _____ _____.

12. He is a *hard* worker.   *Hard* is an _____

      modifying the _____ _____.

13. Angie has a *loose* tooth.   *Loose* is an _____

      modifying the _____ _____.

14. You tied the knot too *loose*.   *Loose* is an _____

      modifying the _____ _____.

15. We applied *late*.   *Late* is an _____

      modifying the _____ _____.

16. Our applications were *late*.   *Late* is an _____

      modifying the _____ _____.

17. You threw *high*.   *High* is an _____

      modifying the _____ _____.

18. Your throw was too *high*.   *High* is an _____

      modifying the _____ _____.

19. The sea was *rough*.   *Rough* is an _____

                                 modifying the _____ _____ .

20. They played *rough*.   *Rough* is an _____

                                 modifying the _____ _____ .

> *Summary:* **Do not jump to the conclusion that a word is an adverb because it ends in *LY*,**
>
> **or that a word is not an adverb because it does not end in *LY*.**
>
> **To tell whether a word is an adverb, or an adjective, or any other part of speech, look at the way the word is used in its sentence.**

lesson 31 Review: Adverbs

Read the following selection:

Lemuel Gulliver often went to sea as a ship's surgeon. He was shipwrecked once in an extremely violent South Sea storm in 1699, and very nearly lost his life, but managed somehow to swim ashore. The land he had come to was not inhabited—at least it seemed so.

For nine hours Gulliver slept soundly on the beach. Awaking, he was greatly surprised to find that he could not move, for he had been firmly tied to the ground by hundreds of very thin strings. He could look only upwards. The sun was unbearably hot.

Soon Gulliver felt something moving on his left leg. It advanced gently towards his chin. Curious, Gulliver bent his eyes downwards and saw that it was a six-inch human, armed with bow and arrow, and followed by about forty similar creatures. So loud did Gulliver roar in astonishment that they ran back instantly. Afterwards Gulliver learned that some had injured themselves seriously as they leaped desperately from his body to the ground.

Gulliver is the main character in *Gulliver's Travels*, an exceptionally exciting novel by Jonathan Swift.

EXERCISE 1. Altogether there are twenty-nine adverbs in the above passage. Adverbs 1–9 and the words they modify are shown in the sample below. List the remaining twenty adverbs and the words they modify, as in the sample.

Sample:

FIRST PARAGRAPH (9 ADVERBS)

1. ADV. *often*   modifies V.   *went.*
2. ADV. *once*   modifies V.   *was shipwrecked.*
3. ADV. *extremely*   modifies ADJ.   *violent.*
4. ADV. *very*   modifies ADV.   *nearly.*
5. ADV. *nearly*   modifies V.   *lost.*
6. ADV. *somehow*   modifies V.   *managed.*
7. ADV. *ashore*   modifies V.   *swim.*
8. ADV. *not*   modifies V.   *was inhabited.*
9. ADV. *so*   modifies V.   *seemed.*

SECOND PARAGRAPH (8 ADVERBS)

10. ADV. _____ modifies _____ _____.

11. ADV. _____ modifies _____ _____.

12. ADV. _____ modifies _____ _____.

13. ADV. _____ modifies _____ _____.

14. ADV. _____ modifies _____ _____.

15. ADV. _____ modifies _____ _____.

16. ADV. _____ modifies _____ _____.

17. ADV. _____ modifies _____ _____.

THIRD PARAGRAPH (11 ADVERBS)

18. ADV. _____ modifies _____ _____.

19. ADV. _____ modifies _____ _____.

20. ADV. _____ modifies _____ _____.

21. ADV. _____ modifies _____ _____.

22. ADV. _____ modifies _____ _____.

23. ADV. _____ modifies _____ _____.

24. ADV. _____ modifies _____ _____.

25. ADV. _____ modifies _____ _____.

26. ADV. _____ modifies _____ _____.

27. ADV. _____ modifies _____ _____.

28. ADV. _____ modifies _____ _____.

LAST PARAGRAPH (1 ADVERB)

29. ADV. _____ modifies _____ _____.

EXERCISE 2. Answer the questions below by writing *adverb* or *adjective* in the space provided.

What do we need to modify

    1. a verb?   An _____.

    2. a noun?   An _____.

    3. an adjective? An _____.

    4. a pronoun?   An _____.

    5. an adverb?   An _____.

EXERCISE 3. Fill the blank with the correct choice.

Sample:

Copy the assignment __*accurately*_____. (*accurate, accurately*)

1. You should take your work _____. (*serious, seriously*)

2. It is _____ cold outside. (*dreadful, dreadfully*)

3. Ripe watermelon tastes _____. (*delicious, deliciously*)

4. They were _____ sorry. (*real, really*)

5. Angela behaved very _____. (*rude, rudely*)

6. Rube has an _____ bad cold. (*unbelievable, unbelievably*)

7. The fire spread _____ quickly. (*awful, awfully*)

8. Rush-hour traffic was _____ slow. (*painful, painfully*)

9. No one plans so _____ as Barbara. (*careful, carefully*)

10. You sounded _____ yesterday. (*hoarse, hoarsely*)

lesson 32 Prepositions

You are supposed to meet with a group of classmates to plan a class party, but you can not remember whether the meeting is

> *before* lunch, or
> *at*   lunch, or
> *after*   lunch.

Others who are supposed to attend are also confused about the exact time of the meeting. The result is that classmates keep arriving at different times, and the meeting is a complete failure.

The outcome could have been altogether different. You and your fellow planners could all have been on time if you had remembered the correct *preposition*.

Question: What is a *preposition?*

We have just been talking about *prepositions. Before, at,* and *after,* in the first sentence of this lesson, are *prepositions.*

Answer: **A *preposition* relates a noun or pronoun to some other part of the sentence.**

Here are some examples of what prepositions do:

1. The group *will meet **before** lunch.*
             V.   PREP.   N.

(The preposition *before* relates the noun *lunch* to the verb *will meet.*)

2. A *letter **for** you* came today.
    N.   PREP. PRON.

(The preposition *for* relates the pronoun *you* to the noun *letter.*)

3. It is *cool **in** the shade.*
     ADJ. PREP.   N.

(The preposition *in* relates the noun *shade* to the adjective *cool.*)

4. The shelf was finished *poorly **along** the edges.*
                ADV.   PREP.   N.

(The preposition *along* relates the noun *edges* to the adverb *poorly.*)

By the way, a few prepositions consist of more than one word: *because of, in spite of,* etc.

5. We were *late **because of** the fog.*
       ADJ.   PREP.   N.

(The preposition *because of* relates the noun *fog* to the adjective *late*.)

Caution: Do not confuse a preposition with an adverb. Compare *before* in the following pair of sentences:

(*a*) We *met **before**.*
         V.   ADV.

(*Before* is an *adverb* modifying the verb *met*.)

(*b*) They *met **before** lunch.*
           V.   PREP.   N.

(*Before* is a *preposition* relating the noun *lunch* to the verb *met*.)

To discover whether a word is a preposition, or an adverb, or any other part of speech, see how it is used in its sentence.

PREPOSITIONS

Here is a list of words commonly used as prepositions:

(If you meet one of the words below in a sentence, check to see that it is in fact being used as a preposition before concluding that it is a preposition. See again sentences *a* and *b*, above.)

about	by	out of
above	despite	outside
across	down	over
after	during	past
against	except	since
along	for	through
among	from	throughout
around	in	till
at	inside	to
because of	in spite of	toward
before	instead of	under
behind	into	until
below	like	up
beside	of	upon
between	off	with
beyond	on	within
but (meaning "except")		without

EXERCISE 1.   Each of the following wise sayings may or may not contain a preposition. If it contains a preposition, write that preposition in the space provided. If it does not, write *no prep*.

Samples:

Do not put all your eggs in one basket.   *in*

The early bird catches the worm.   *no prep.*

1. A word to the wise is sufficient.   _____

2. Money is the root of all evil.   _____

3. Those who laugh last laugh best.   _____

4. Do not judge a book by its cover.   _____

5. Great oaks from little acorns grow.   _____

6. Rome was not built in a day.   _____

7. Charity begins at home.   _____

8. Fools and their money are soon parted.   _____

9. An apple never falls far from the tree.   _____

10. There is nothing so comfortable as an old shoe.   _____

11. Birds of a feather flock together.   _____

12. A house divided against itself can not stand.   _____

13. Pride goeth before destruction.   _____

14. Better late than never.   _____

15. People who live in glass houses should not throw stones.   _____

16. Time and tide wait for no man.   _____

17. Do not put off until tomorrow what you can do today.   _____

18. You cannot make a silk purse out of a sow's ear.   _____

19. He who hesitates is lost.   _____

20. Necessity is the mother of invention.   _____

EXERCISE 2.   Change each sentence to a sentence that has the opposite meaning—and do this by changing just one word, the *preposition*, to another preposition.

Sample:

The customer wanted coffee *with* cream.

The customer wanted coffee _____*without*_____ cream.

1. We waited *outside* the library.

   We waited _____ the library.

2. Most of my classmates voted *for* me.

   Most of my classmates voted _____ me.

3. Take one tablet *before* each meal.

   Take one tablet _____ each meal.

4. I went *up* the stairs.

   I went _____ the stairs.

5. Place the right hand *over* the left.

   Place the right hand _____ the left.

6. Here is a gift *from* Susan.

   Here is a gift _____ Susan.

7. Did someone run *into* the house?

   Did someone run _____ the house?

8. Yesterday's temperature was *above* normal.

   Yesterday's temperature was _____ normal.

9. The trip *to* school took an hour.

   The trip _____ school took an hour.

10. Most of the fans were *against* us.

    Most of the fans were _____ us.

You have probably noticed by now that every preposition is followed by a noun or a pronoun.

He slammed the ball ***out of*** the ***infield***.
                    PREP.   N.

Please do not leave ***without us***.
                 PREP.   PRON.

Let us now give our attention to the noun or pronoun that follows a preposition.

Object of the Preposition

The noun or pronoun that follows a preposition is known as the *object of the preposition*.

He slammed the ball *out of* the **_infield_**.
          PREP.   OBJ. OF PREP.

(The noun *infield* is the object of the preposition *out of.*)

Please do not leave *without* **_us_**.
        PREP.   OBJ. OF PREP.

(The pronoun *us* is the object of the preposition *without.*)

EXERCISE 3. Find the *preposition* and the *object of the preposition.*

Samples:

	PREP.	OBJ. OF PREP.
Who was behind the wheel?	*behind*	*wheel*
Because of you, we could not go.	*Because of*	*you*

1. The story is about a teenager.
2. Get out of this house!
3. Meet me outside the library.
4. She has been ill since Friday.
5. Wait until next week.
6. Do you want bread instead of a roll?
7. Everyone agreed except Ralph.
8. Drop the letter in the nearest mailbox.
9. Play continued in spite of the snow.
10. I have never seen anything like it.

lesson 33 Prepositional Phrases

All of us have been using *prepositional phrases* since early childhood. Every day we encounter hundreds of prepositional phrases when we listen, read, or write, and we use them very frequently when we speak. Take, for example, the story of a "lost" wristwatch—almost everyone of us has had such an experience—in which we tell how we looked

> *in our pockets* (or *in our purse*),
> *on the dresser,*
> *under the sofa,*
> *between the cushions,*

and how we finally found it

> *on our wrist.*

All of the italicized expressions above are *prepositional phrases.*

What Is a Prepositional Phrase?

A *prepositional phrase* is a group of words that

(1) begins with a *preposition*, and

(2) ends with the *object of the preposition* (a noun or pronoun).

EXAMPLE OF A PREPOSITIONAL PHRASE ENDING WITH A NOUN:

> I wrote **with a pen**.
>   PREP. PHR.

(The prepositional phrase *with a pen* begins with
the preposition *with* and ends with the noun *pen.*
The noun *pen* is the object of the preposition *with.*)

A word that modifies the object of the preposition is considered part of the prepositional phrase:

> I wrote **with a new pen**.
>   PREP. PHR.

(The adjective *new* modifies the noun *pen* and is a
part of the prepositional phrase.)

Without her, they would have lost the game.
PREP. PHR.

(The prepositional phrase *Without her* consists of the preposition *without* and the pronoun *her*. The pronoun *her* is the object of the preposition *without*.)

EXERCISE 1. Underline the prepositional phrase. Then, in the spaces at the right, enter the *preposition* and the *object of the preposition*.

Sample:

	PREP.	OBJ. OF PREP.
I bought a ticket for the first performance.	*for*	*performance*
1. A road runs along the river.		
2. Let us meet at the bus stop.		
3. With your help we cannot fail.		
4. A remark by your brother hurt me very much.		
5. The Jacksons live above us.		
6. Take the train instead of the bus.		
7. No one knew the answer but Nina.		
8. Nathaniel swims like a fish.		
9. Who was sitting beside you?		
10. In spite of her failure, she will try again.		

Composition Hint

Sometimes we can express an idea either through an adverb or a prepositional phrase.

Handle the glassware *carefully*.
ADV.

Handle the glassware *with care*.
PREP. PHR.

If you know more than one way to express your ideas, you will be a better writer.

EXERCISE 2.   Replace the italicized adverb with a prepositional phrase.

Samples:

He acted *selfishly*.   *in a selfish manner*

Luckily, the bus was waiting.   *By luck*

You cannot stay *here*.   *in this place*

1. Does the motor run *quietly?*   _____
2. It happened *accidentally*.   _____
3. Who lives *there?*   _____
4. She replied *angrily*.   _____
5. We worry *always*.   _____
6. The child slept *restlessly*.   _____
7. You are *doubtlessly* right.   _____
8. Few of us face danger *fearlessly*.   _____
9. The meetings are conducted *democratically*. _____
10. *Instantly*, the fire was extinguished.   _____

Another Composition Hint

Sometimes we can express an idea either through an adjective or a prepositional phrase.

An unsigned check is ***valueless***.
ADJ.

An unsigned check is ***of no value***.
PREP. PHR.

EXERCISE 3.   Rewrite the sentence, replacing the italicized adjective with a prepositional phrase.

Samples:

You may find yourself *penniless*.
  You may find yourself without a penny.

A mayor is an *important* person.
  A mayor is a person of importance.

1. Many *European* tourists visit the United States each year.

_____

2. My help was *useless*.

_____

3. Most cars use *unleaded* gasoline.

_____

4. We are on good terms with the *Canadian* people.

_____

5. Take the *end* seat.

_____

EXERCISE 4. One of the most admired short poems in our literature is "Fog" by Carl Sandburg.

> The fog comes
> on little cat feet.
>
> It sits looking
> over harbor and city
> on silent haunches
> and then moves on.

Questions:

1. In which prepositional phrase does Carl Sandburg tell

   (*a*) how the fog comes?   _____ _____ _____ _____

   (*b*) how the fog sits?   _____ _____ _____

   (*c*) where the fog looks?   _____ _____ _____ _____

2. What part of speech is the last word of the poem?   _____

lesson 34 Conjunctions

This lesson deals mainly with three simple but very important words:

> *and,*
> *but*, and
> *or.*

These words belong to a group called *conjunctions*.

What Is a Conjunction?

A *conjunction* is a word that connects other words or groups of words.

The most common conjunctions are *and, but,* and *or*.

What Are Some Examples of the Work That Conjunctions Do?

1. A conjunction connects *nouns:*

Milk **and** cheese are dairy products.
N.   CONJ.   N.

(The conjunction *and* connects the nouns *milk* and *cheese*.)

Ruth, Joe,   **or**   Tom will lead the discussion.
N.   N.   CONJ.   N.

(The conjunction *or* connects the nouns *Ruth, Joe,* and *Tom*.)

2. A conjunction connects *adjectives:*

The winners were *tired* **but** *happy*.
ADJ. CONJ. ADJ.

(The conjunction *but* connects the adjectives *tired* and *happy*.)

3. A conjunction connects *verbs:*

I do not care if I *win*   **or**   *lose*.
V.   CONJ.   V.

(The conjunction *or* connects the verbs *win* and *lose*.)

4. A conjunction connects *pronouns*, or a *noun and a pronoun*:

You *and* she are always on time.
PRON. CONJ. PRON.

(The conjunction *and* connects the pronouns *You* and *she*.)

Alex *and* I are neighbors.
N.   CONJ. PRON.

(The conjunction *and* connects the noun *Alex* and the pronoun *I*.)

5. A conjunction connects *adverbs*:

It rained *gently* **but** *steadily*.
ADV. CONJ.   ADV.

(The conjunction *but* connects the adverbs *gently* and *steadily*.)

6. A conjunction connects *prepositional phrases*:

Park *on Washington Street*   **or**   *on the driveway*.
PREP. PHR.   CONJ.   PREP. PHR.

(The conjunction *or* connects the prepositional phrases *on Washington Street* and *on the driveway*.)

In addition to the above, conjunctions can make still other connections, as we shall see later.

EXERCISE 1. Find the conjunction and explain what it connects.

Sample:

You are improving slowly but surely.

The conjunction ___*but*___ connects the _____*adverbs*_____

_____*slowly*_____ and _____*surely*_____.

1. We were warm and comfortable.

The conjunction _____ connects the _____

_____ and _____.

2. She and I do not get along.

The conjunction _____ connects the _____

_____ and _____.

3. The meal was delicious but inexpensive.

The conjunction _____ connects the _____

_____ and _____.

4. Yolanda or Sue will collect the tickets.

The conjunction _____ connects the _____

_____ and _____.

5. Jim called at noon and in the evening.

The conjunction _____ connects the _____

_____ and _____.

6. The manager politely but firmly asked us to leave.

The conjunction _____ connects the _____

_____ and _____.

7. Would Randy and you care to join us?

The conjunction _____ connects the _____ _____

and the _____ _____.

8. Prices may go up or down.

The conjunction _____ connects the _____

_____ and _____.

9. The storm battered Texas and Louisiana.

The conjunction _____ connects the _____

_____ and _____.

Composition Hint

The conjunctions **and, or,** and **but** connect words or expressions of equal rank: two nouns, two adjectives, two adverbs, two prepositional phrases, etc.

POOR: They worked *quickly* and *with care*.

(The words connected are not of equal rank: *quickly* is an adverb, and *with care* is a prepositional phrase.)

BETTER: They worked *quickly* and *carefully*.

(The words connected are of equal rank: *quickly* and *carefully* are adverbs.)

However, as we have seen on page 136, a conjunction can connect a noun and a pronoun.

CORRECT: *Mary* and *I* will help.
     N.   PRON.

Whenever you write, watch your use of the conjunctions **and, or,** and **but** to see that they connect words or expressions of equal rank.

EXERCISE 2. Rewrite the sentence if the words connected by the conjunction are not of the same rank. If they are of the same rank, write "correct."

Samples:

Donna was tired and in an angry mood.
Donna was tired and angry.

My neighbor and I are sports fans.
Correct

1. We were treated decently and with fairness.

2. The problem has been discussed frequently and in a thorough manner.

3. The ball bounced off the fence and into the bushes.

4. Was the play successful or a failure?

5. Many thought I was a fool and unwise.

6. Tomorrow will be sunny but windy.

7. Frank spoke briefly but with effectiveness.

8. Your brother or you must have left the door open.

9. Did the pain come suddenly or in a gradual manner?

10. Their struggle seemed endless and without hope.

Combining Simple Sentences

Another use for the conjunctions **and, but,** and **or** is to combine *simple sentences* into *compound sentences.*

A *simple sentence* has only one subject and one verb.

<u>**Paul**</u> <u>**washed**</u> the dishes. <u>**I**</u> <u>**dried**</u> them. (*simple sentences*)
  S.   V.   S.   V.

A *compound sentence* consists of two or more simple sentences joined by *and, but,* or *or*.

<u>**Paul washed the dishes**</u>, and <u>**I dried them.**</u> (*compound sentence*)
  simple sentence   CONJ.   simple sentence

Punctuation: A comma [,] usually precedes the conjunction.

Use the conjunction **but** to combine simple sentences that contrast with each other.

The <u>**boat**</u> <u>**overturned**</u>. <u>**Nobody**</u> <u>**was**</u> injured. (*simple sentences*)
      S.   V.   S.   V.

<u>**The boat overturned**</u>, but <u>**nobody was injured**</u>. (*compound sentence*)
  simple sentence   CONJ.   simple sentence

Use the conjunction **or** to combine simple sentences expressing a choice between two or more possibilities.

<u>**I**</u> <u>**will bring**</u> my basketball. <u>**We**</u> <u>**can use**</u> yours. (*simple sentences*)
  S.   V.   S.   V.

<u>**I will bring my basketball**</u>, or <u>**we can use yours**</u>. (*compound sentence*)
  simple sentence   CONJ.   simple sentence

EXERCISE 3. Using **and, but,** or **or**, combine each pair of simple sentences into a compound sentence.

Samples:

We took along warm clothing. It was not needed.
  We took along warm clothing, but it was not needed.

The weather was fine. We had a good time.
  The weather was fine, and we had a good time.

Is cash required? Is a check acceptable?
  Is cash required, or is a check acceptable?

1. Lightning appeared in the distance. Raindrops began to fall.

2. The engine needs a tuning. The brakes have to be relined.

3. We called Steven. He was not at home.

4. Are you pleased with the merchandise? Do you want a refund?

5. Stan offered me his notes. I did not take them.

6. Rhoda is running for president. I am her campaign manager.

7. Ted wrote to Mona. She did not answer.

8. Amy shut off the water. The house would have been flooded.

9. Alex apologized to me. We shook hands.

10. I warned you. You did not listen.

lesson 35 Interjections

An *interjection* is a word or short expression that shows sudden strong feeling.

Oh! The toast is burning!
interj.

Oops! I nearly fell.
   interj.

Good grief! Look what happened!
       interj.

An interjection is considered as a unit in itself and is not tied grammatically to any other word in the sentence. *Oh!* in the first example is like a sentence by itself. The same is true of *Oops!* and *Good grief!*

Punctuation: An interjection is usually followed by an *exclamation point* [!]. However, if the interjection is a mild one, it is followed by a *comma* [,]; the comma separates it from the rest of the sentence.

Oh, excuse me.
interj.

An exclamatory sentence often follows an interjection.

Good grief! Look what happened!
   interj.   exclamatory sentence

EXERCISE 1. What would you say in each of the following situations? Choose your answer from the suggested replies at the end of the exercise, and write it in the space provided.

Sample:

Your coach announces that the team is getting new uniforms.

Wow! That's great!

1. Someone tells you that you have won a thousand dollars.

   _____

2. You mop the sweat from your face with a handkerchief.

   _____

3. Someone for whom you have been waiting finally arrives.

   _____

4. The cat overturns your oatmeal and orange juice.

   _____

5. Someone knocks. Opening the door, you are mildly disgusted to find it is a person who has been pestering you.

   _____

6. Arriving at the pool, you find that you have left some essential equipment at home.

   _____

7. Someone accidentally steps on your painful toe.

   _____

8. You see a $1.29 price tag on a bicycle. The dealer explains it is an error.

   _____

9. A good friend invites you to a party, but you have already made another appointment.

   _____

10. Someone in a restaurant puts on your coat and is about to walk out with it.

    _____

SUGGESTED REPLIES

Ugh! What a mess!   Oh, it's you again.
Baloney! I don't believe it.   Man! It's hot in here!
Gee, I can't make it.   Ouch! That hurts!
Hey! That's mine!   Well! You got here at last!
Gosh! I forgot my swimsuit.   Aha, I thought so.

Read the following conversation:

> Hey, Henry. I'm quitting.
> Shucks! Why, Joe?
> I don't think the boss likes me.
> Nonsense! What put that into your head?
> I have a feeling I'm not wanted around here.
> Oh, you're imagining things.
> Well, maybe. But I don't seem to do anything right. I just ruined a couple of boards. Yesterday I brought the wrong nails, and before that I cut my hand. Golly, I feel useless.
> Joe, be sensible. For goodness sakes! How do you suppose I learned? I made lots of mistakes when I started. Everyone around here knows you're a trainee.
> But I'm so dumb and clumsy.
> Hogwash! Don't you believe it.
> You're a swell guy, Joe. I guess I'll give it another try.
> Great!
> Ouch! I just banged my finger.

EXERCISE 2. There are ten interjections in the conversation you have just read. List them in the spaces below in the order in which they appear.

1. _____   6. _____
2. _____   7. _____
3. _____   8. _____
4. _____   9. _____
5. _____   10. _____

EXERCISE 3. What part of speech is the italicized word?

> *Reminder:* **To determine what part of speech a word is, check to see how that word is used in its sentence.**

Samples:

A *man* answered the telephone.   _noun_

Man the oars.   _verb_

Man! Was I angry!   _interjection_

1. *Fire!* Everybody out!   _____
2. Can the firm *fire* you for no reason?   _____
3. The *fire* was brought under control.   _____

4. Pollution is a *great* problem.   _____

5. *Great!* I'll be there in a minute.   _____

6. The *well* ran dry.   _____

7. *Well*, are we ready?   _____

8. Marge swims *well*.   _____

9. Did you ever hear such *nonsense?*   _____

10. *Nonsense!* You're all wrong.   _____

INDEX

INDEX

compound subject:
  to avoid repetition, 27, 74
  to avoid unnecessary words, 74
  composition hint involving compound
    subjects, 27, 74
  compound subject and compound verb, 30
  definition, 27
  punctuation, 28
  uses fewer words, 27, 74

compound verb:
  to avoid repetition of the subject, 30
  composition hint involving compound verb,
    30
  compound subject and compound verb, 30
  definition, 30
  punctuation, 31

conjunctions:
  and, but, and *or,* 135–140
  composition hint involving conjunctions, 137
  connect words of equal rank, 137
  definition, 135

consonants, 48

contraction:
  definition, 76
  differentiated from possessive pronoun, 78
  pronoun in, 76–78
  verb in, 76–78, 90–93

D

declarative sentence:
  definition, 5
  most sentences are declarative, 5
  punctuation, 5

direct object:
  compound, 62, 74
  definition, 60
  procedure for finding, 62
  pronoun as direct object and indirect object,
    72, 73, 74

E

exclamation point:
  at end of exclamatory sentence, 9
  at end of imperative sentence, 8
  at end of interjection, 141

exclamatory sentence:
  definition, 9
  follows an interjection, 141
  punctuation, 9

F

formal English:
  use complete sentences, 1, 25
  avoid contractions, 91–93

G

grammar, 34

H

helping verb:
  definition, 85
  list, 86
  subject follows first helping verb in a
    question, 87

I

imperative sentence:
  definition, 8
  punctuation, 8
  You, as understood subject, 8

incomplete sentence:
  in informal English, 1, 25
  subject and part of predicate omitted, 1–4,
    24–26

indirect object:
  comes before direct object, 65
  compound indirect object, 74
  definition, 65
  noun as indirect object, 65–68
  pronoun as indirect object, 72, 73, 74

informal English:
  contraction in, 77, 91
  incomplete sentence in, 1, 25

interjection:
  definition, 141
  punctuation, 141

interrogative sentence:
  definition, 6
  punctuation, 6

L

linking verb:
  be as a test for a linking verb, 83–84
  complement of a linking verb, 100
  definition, 82
  distinguished from action verb, 83–84
  how to recognize, 83–84
  list, 82–83
  predicate adjective after a linking verb, 102–
    103
  predicate noun after a linking verb, 103–106

ly:
  added to an adjective to form an adverb, 115–
    118
  word ending in *ly* may or may not be an
    adverb, 122

M

main verb, 85

modifier:
  adjective, 94–98
  adverb, 110–114
  defined, 94